Oxford Skills World

Listening 6

WITH Speaking

Joanna Ross

OXFORD

UNIVERSITY PRESS

OXFORD
UNIVERSITY PRESS

198 Madison Avenue
New York, NY 10016 USA

Great Clarendon Street, Oxford, OX2 6DP, United Kingdom

Oxford University Press is a department of the University of Oxford.
It furthers the University's objective of excellence in research, scholarship,
and education by publishing worldwide. Oxford is a registered trade
mark of Oxford University Press in the UK and in certain other countries

© Oxford University Press 2019

The moral rights of the author have been asserted

First published in 2019

2023 2022 2021 2020 2019

10 9 8 7 6 5 4 3 2 1

No unauthorized photocopying

ISBN: 978 0 19 411344 1 STUDENT BOOK WITH WORKBOOK

Printed in China

This book is printed on paper from certified and well-managed sources

ACKNOWLEDGMENTS

Cover illustration and main character illustrations by: Shane McGowan/The
Organisation

Cover photograph: Johnathan Knowles/Getty

Back cover photograph: Oxford University Press building/David Fisher

Student Book

Illustrations by: Scott Angle pp.32, 50–51, 82–84; Peter Francis/MB Artists pp.14,
22, 38; 5W Infographics pp.36t, 40; Anthony Lewis/MB Artists pp.8, 44–45,
64; Julissa Mora pp.23, 24, 46, 74; Juan Moreno/MB Artists pp.16, 36–37, 88;
Christos Skaltsas/Advocate Art pp.12–13, 72; Jomike Tejido/MB Artists pp.30,
52, 78–80, 86

*The Publishers would like to thank the following for their kind permission to reproduce
photographs and other copyright material*: 123rf: pp.26 (firefighter takling
blaze/Claude Beaubien), (dangerous wooden bridge/ryzhkovoleksandr),
43 (traveller in airport/David Prado), 57 (bag being placed on conveyor/Geza
Farkas), 68 (tumble dryer/Kichigin Aleksandr); Alamy: pp.9 (US post office
exterior/Francis Vachon), 43 (boy in Paris/Sergey Novikov), 71 (boy planting
seeds/Catalin Petolea), (girl cycling/MovieAboutYou); Getty: pp.10 (woman
asking for directions/kokouu), 15 (toy shop window/Tim Hall), (two different
shops/Busà Photography), (people on crosswalk/urbancow), 17 (two boys
running/KOICHI SAITO/a.collectionRF), 29 (girl waving from car/BJI/Blue
Jean Images), 31 (boy watching butterfly/Mint Images), 40 (video call with
baby/Emma Kim), 57 (children waiting in departure lounge/stockstudiox),
68 (carrots/mrod), (changing lightbulb/Floresco Productions), (waving from
train window/Vladimir Vladimirov), (girl sleeping/D. Sharon Pruitt Pink
Sherbet Photography), 70 (woman cycling/olaser), 76–77 (vintage video game/
Maxiphoto), 85 (boy flying drone/Miguel Sotomayor), (children in computer
class/gradyreese), 87 (girl with virtual reality headset/Steve Debenport);
Oxford University Press: pp.6–7 (busy intersection/Shutterstock/Sean Pavone),
56 (plane taking off/Shutterstock), 67 (bottle bird feeder/Shutterstock/Maxal
Tamor), 81 (curry and rice/Shutterstock/vm2002); Shutterstock: pp.11 (boy on
bicycle/Spotmatik Ltd), 15 (boy riding bicycle/Brian A Jackson), 18 (boy sitting
in tree/Fotoluminate LLC), 20–21 (identical twins/Lyubov Levitskaya), 25 (beach
and mountains/TasfotoNL), 26 (four children/Monkey Business Images), (lonely
boy/wavebreakmedia), (two friends/Monkey Business Images), 27 (broken
window/Marina N. Mak), 28 (father and son/pixelheadphoto digitalskillet),
29 (children playing chess/Karen Struthers), (leaping cat/Grigorita Ko), (baby/
Daniel_Dash), 34–35 (parents with baby/pixelheadphoto digitalskillet),
39 (floating market/nimon), 40 (Greek coastal village/leoks), (smartphone/
Georgejmclittle), (Neschwanstein castle/Yury Dmitrienko), 41 (teenager
listening to music/PONG HANDSOME), 42 (train emerging from tunnel/T.W.
van Urk), 43 (Thai food stall/saiko3p), (Greek beach/Adisa), 48–49 (Iguassu
fall/R.M. Nunes), 53 (scuba divers/Richard Whitcombe), 54 (teenager at check
in desk/Ekaterina Pokrovsky), (man looking at watch/Elnur), (currency
exchange/Ton Anurak), (boy waiting with luggage/plantic), (woman handing
over passport/Pressmaster), 55 (busy airport/structuresxx), 57 (woman seated
on plane/leungchopan), (currency exchange/Sorbis), 58 (sun terrace/thipjang),
(white water rafting/Strahil Dimitrov), (inside cave house/LiskaM), (hot air
ballooning/Tatiana Popova), 59 (aerial view of Rio/Celso Diniz), 60 (chairlift in
Gauja/Viesturs Jugs), 62–63 (bug hotel in forest/Alexandru Cristian Martin),
64 (plastic pollution in water/Rich Carey), (recycling plastic bottle/CAT
SCAPE), 65 (plastic carton planters/SewCream), 66 (recycling bins/Unchalee
Khun), 68 (dishwasher/Yunava1), 69 (laundry on clothes line/Fesus Robert),
71 (turning tap off/BlurryMe), (jean bag/gowithstock), 73 (tending to vegetable
patch/ivan_kislitsin), 76–77 (modern video game/Bloomicon), 82 (Ba/Rawpixel.
com), (Bb/TAKLONGKORAT), (Bc/Andrey_Popov), (Bd/Georgejmclittle), 85 (girl
taking selfie/cheapbooks), (robot walking/Phonlamai Photo)

Workbook

Illustrations by: Scott Angle p.95; Peter Francis/MB Artists pp.99, 107; Julissa
Mora p.93; Christos Skaltsas/Advocate Art p.113; Jomike Tejido/MB Artists
p.103

*The Publishers would like to thank the following for their kind permission to reproduce
photographs and other copyright material*: 123rf: p.105 (mountain at sunrise/
Maurizio Biso); Alamy: pp.91 (traditional Turkish restaurant/Yavuz Sariyildiz),
111 (farmer collecting hen's eggs/Wavebreak Media); Oxford University Press:
pp.101 (packet of potato chips/Shutterstock/Yalcin Sonat), 109 (plastic rubbish
on beach/Shutterstock/Rich Carey); Shutterstock: p.97 (doctor and young
patient/ESB Professional)

Table of Contents

Hi! I'm Olly.

Hi, I'm Molly!

Introduction

Welcome to Oxford Skills World

Oxford Skills World: Listening with Speaking is a flexible paired skills course that takes students on a journey toward independent learning, providing them with strategies and support to reach their goals.

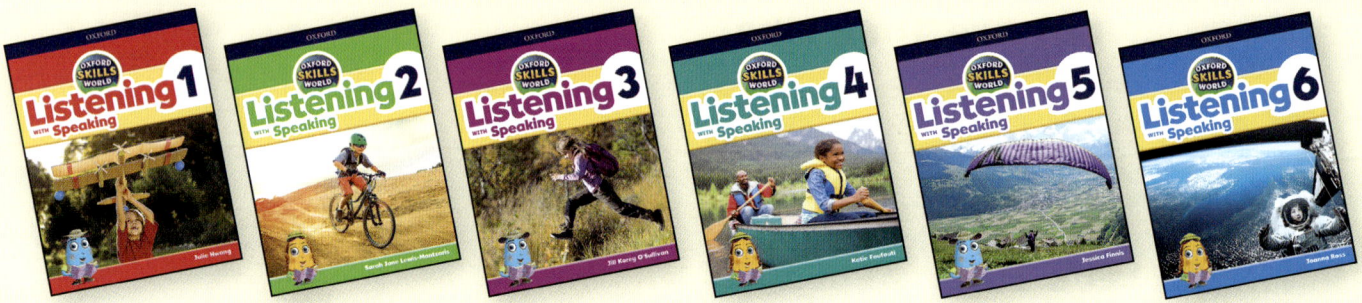

For Students

- Student Book / Workbook
- Student's website with downloadable audio and extra resources
  www.oup.com/elt/oxfordskillsworld

For Teachers

- Downloadable Teacher's Pack with instructional support, assessment, professional development videos, projects, and speaking resources
- Classroom Presentation Tool
- Teacher's website with downloadable audio and extra resources
  www.oup.com/elt/teacher/oxfordskillsworld

Be the Leader on Your Skills Adventure!

Hi! We're Olly and Molly, your skills adventure guides. We help you reach your goals by introducing new listening and speaking strategies, asking helpful questions, and giving friendly reminders. Most importantly, we cheer you on every step of the way! Let's go!

Quick Guide

Inside Each Topic

Topic Opener

Theme-based topics provide high-interest content relevant to students' lives.

My Goals introduces students to the objectives of each unit in the topic.*

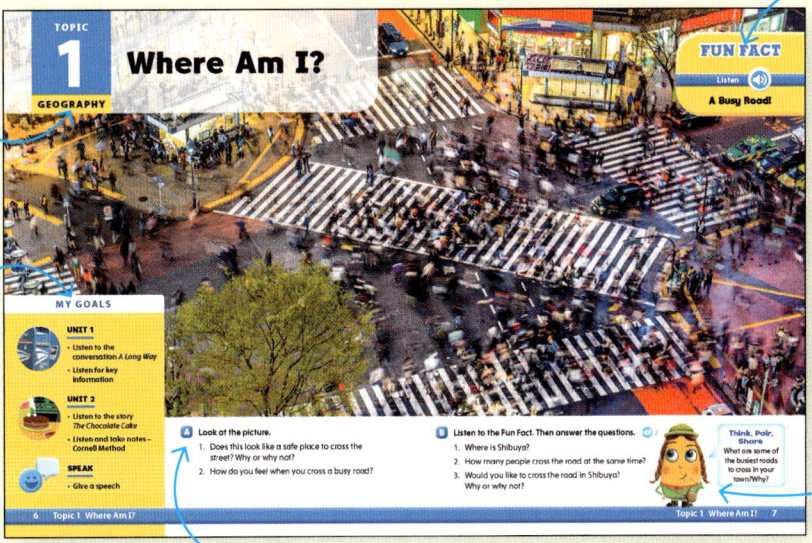

Students listen to a Fun Fact to increase their engagement with the topic.

Fun characters, Olly and Molly, encourage 21st century skills like critical thinking, collaboration, and communication.

Students answer questions to activate prior knowledge and think critically.

Get Ready to Listen • Listen

Students learn and practice new vocabulary. They can look up unknown words in a dictionary at the back of the book.

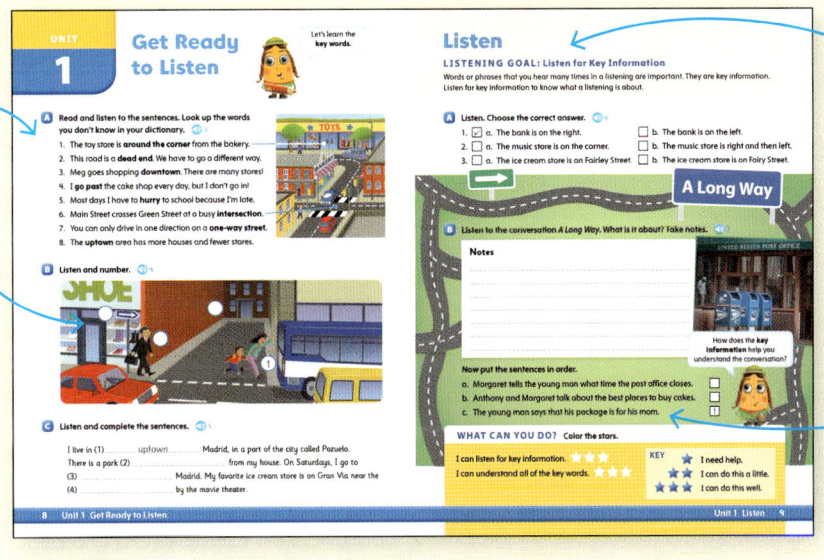

Listening Goals are strategies students can apply to any passage.

Students apply strategies to high-interest fiction and nonfiction passages, think critically about what they hear, and make connections to their own lives.

*Each topic contains two thematically related units.

Quick Guide

Understand

Students increase their comprehension of the passages by applying listening strategies to what they have heard.

Students complete activities focused on listening comprehension and critical thinking.

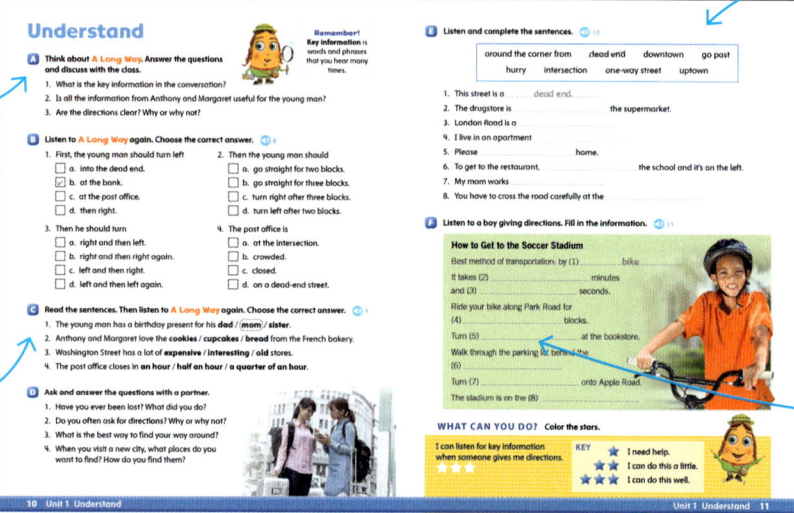

Vocabulary application activities strengthen students' comprehension of the unit's new language.

Additional passages and activities prepare students for task types found on standardized exams, such as Cambridge English Qualifications for young learners.

Listening Check

With helpful reminders from Olly and Molly, students apply the **Listening Goals** from both units to a new passage.

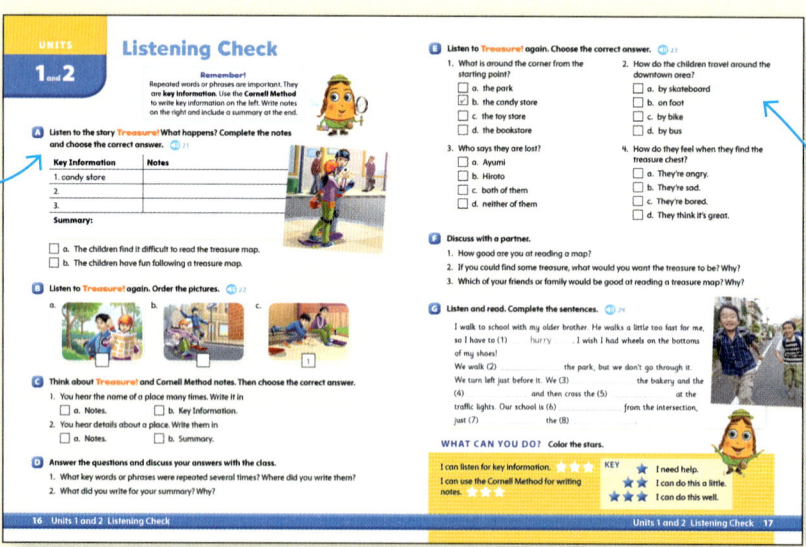

Students complete activities to boost listening comprehension and vocabulary application.

Get Ready to Speak • Speak

Speaking Goals prepare students to speak in different contexts.

Speaking Tips provide guidance on grammar, punctuation, and mechanics and help students speak fluently and accurately.

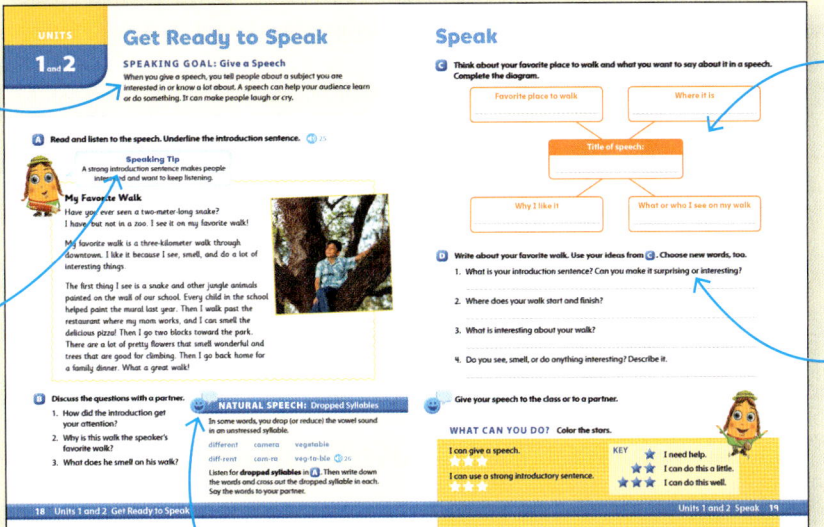

Students use graphic organizers to organize their thoughts for their own speaking.

Thought-provoking questions help students generate ideas they will use in their own speaking.

Natural Speech tips help students listen for and use natural rhythm, pronunciation, and intonation.

Workbook

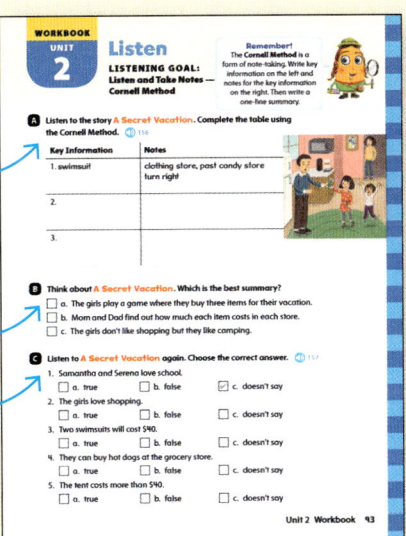

Workbook pages at the end of the book provide more opportunities for students to apply their **Listening Goals** and boost comprehension.

Additional activities provide extra opportunities for listening comprehension and vocabulary practice.

Students apply the topic's **Speaking Tip** to ensure proper usage in their own speaking.

Where Am I?

MY GOALS

UNIT 1

- Listen to the conversation *A Long Way*
- Listen for key information

UNIT 2

- Listen to the story *The Chocolate Cake*
- Listen and take notes – Cornell Method

SPEAK

- Give a speech

 Look at the picture.

1. Does this look like a safe place to cross the street? Why or why not?

2. How do you feel when you cross a busy road?

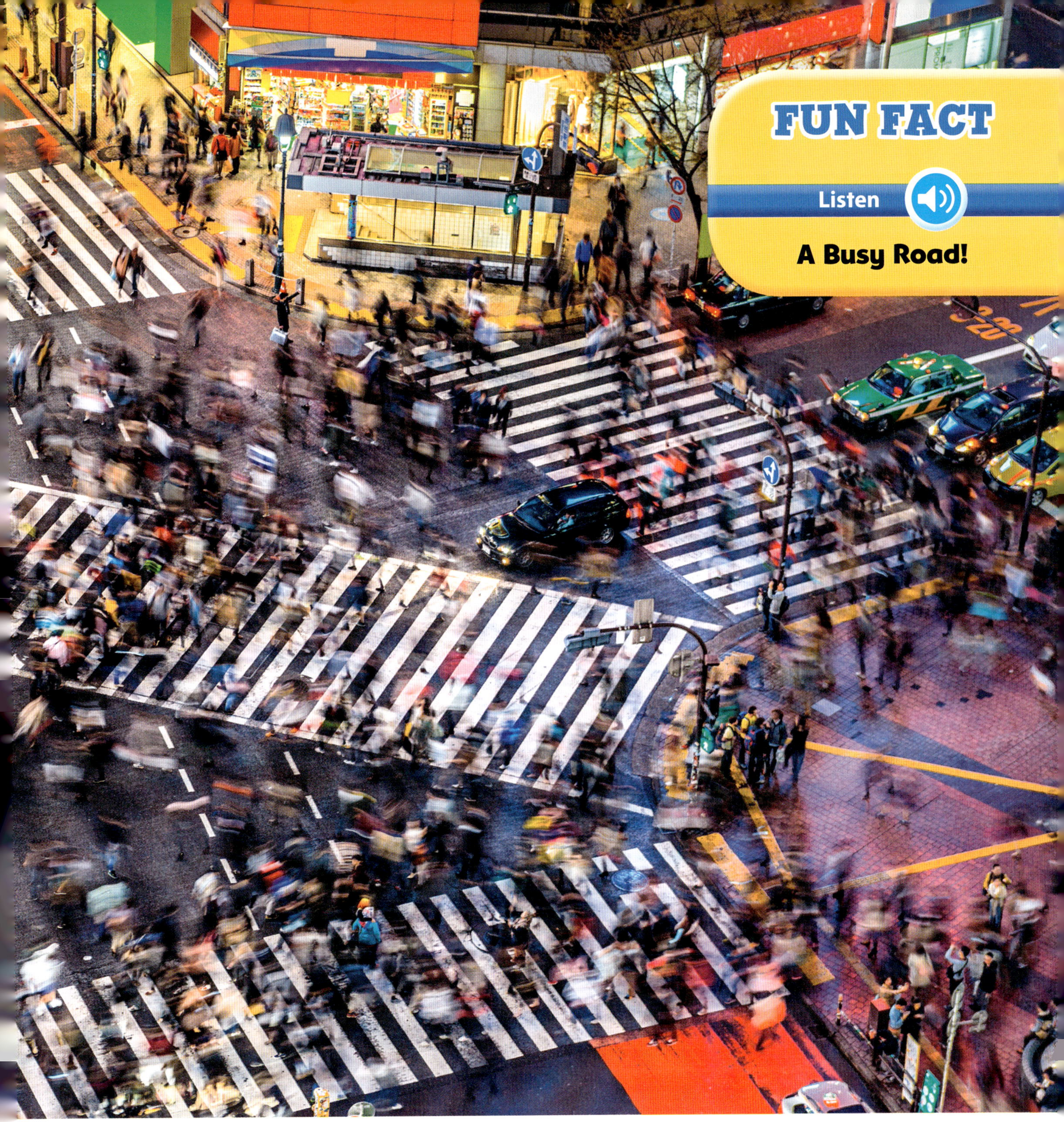

FUN FACT

Listen

A Busy Road!

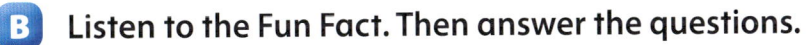

B Listen to the Fun Fact. Then answer the questions. 2

1. Where is Shibuya?
2. How many people cross the road at the same time?
3. Would you like to cross the road in Shibuya? Why or why not?

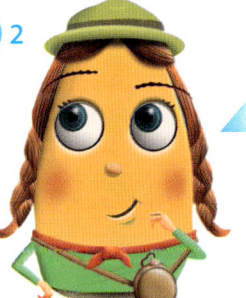

Think, Pair, Share
What are some of the busiest roads to cross in your town? Why?

Get Ready to Listen

Let's learn the **key words**.

A Read and listen to the sentences. Look up the words you don't know in your dictionary. 🔊 3

1. The toy store is **around the corner** from the bakery.
2. This road is a **dead end**. We have to go a different way.
3. Meg goes shopping **downtown**. There are many stores!
4. I **go past** the cake shop every day, but I don't go in!
5. Most days I have to **hurry** to school because I'm late.
6. Main Street crosses Green Street at a busy **intersection**.
7. You can only drive in one direction on a **one-way street**.
8. The **uptown** area has more houses and fewer stores.

B Listen and number. 🔊 4

C Listen and complete the sentences. 🔊 5

I live in (1) _____uptown_____ Madrid, in a part of the city called Pozuelo.

There is a park (2) _____ from my house. On Saturdays, I go to

(3) _____ Madrid. My favorite ice cream store is on Gran Via near the

(4) _____ by the movie theater.

Listen

LISTENING GOAL: Listen for Key Information

Words or phrases that you hear many times in a listening are important. They are key information.
Listen for key information to know what a listening is about.

A Listen. Choose the correct answer. 🔊 6

1. ☑ a. The bank is on the right.   ☐ b. The bank is on the left.
2. ☐ a. The music store is on the corner.   ☐ b. The music store is right and then left.
3. ☐ a. The ice cream store is on Fairley Street.   ☐ b. The ice cream store is on Fairy Street.

A Long Way

B Listen to the conversation *A Long Way*. What is it about? Take notes. 🔊 7

UNITED STATES POST OFFICE

Notes

_____
_____
_____
_____
_____
_____
_____

How does the **key information** help you understand the conversation?

Now put the sentences in order.

a. Margaret tells the young man what time the post office closes. ☐
b. Anthony and Margaret talk about the best places to buy cakes. ☐
c. The young man says that his package is for his mom. ☐ 1

WHAT CAN YOU DO?   Color the stars.

I can listen for key information. ★ ★ ★

I can understand all of the key words. ★ ★ ★

KEY

★ I need help.

★ ★ I can do this a little.

★ ★ ★ I can do this well.

Understand

A Think about **A Long Way**. Answer the questions and discuss with the class.

1. What is the key information in the conversation?

2. Is all the information from Anthony and Margaret useful for the young man?

3. Are the directions clear? Why or why not?

B Listen to **A Long Way** again. Choose the correct answer.  8

1. First, the young man should turn left
   - ☐ a. into the dead end.
   - ✔ b. at the bank.
   - ☐ c. at the post office.
   - ☐ d. then right.

2. Then the young man should
   - ☐ a. go straight for two blocks.
   - ☐ b. go straight for three blocks.
   - ☐ c. turn right after three blocks.
   - ☐ d. turn left after two blocks.

3. Then he should turn
   - ☐ a. right and then left.
   - ☐ b. right and then right again.
   - ☐ c. left and then right.
   - ☐ d. left and then left again.

4. The post office is
   - ☐ a. at the intersection.
   - ☐ b. crowded.
   - ☐ c. closed.
   - ☐ d. on a dead-end street.

C Read the sentences. Then listen to **A Long Way** again. Choose the correct answer. 9

1. The young man has a birthday present for his **dad** / **mom** / **sister**.

2. Anthony and Margaret love the **cookies** / **cupcakes** / **bread** from the French bakery.

3. Washington Street has a lot of **expensive** / **interesting** / **old** stores.

4. The post office closes in **an hour** / **half an hour** / **a quarter of an hour**.

D Ask and answer the questions with a partner.

1. Have you ever been lost? What did you do?

2. Do you often ask for directions? Why or why not?

3. What is the best way to find your way around?

4. When you visit a new city, what places do you want to find? How do you find them?

E Listen and complete the sentences. 🔊 10

| around the corner from | ~~dead end~~ | downtown | go past |
| hurry | intersection | one-way street | uptown |

1. This street is a _____ dead end. _____

2. The drugstore is _____ the supermarket.

3. London Road is a _____

4. I live in an apartment _____

5. Please _____ home.

6. To get to the restaurant, _____ the school and it's on the left.

7. My mom works _____

8. You have to cross the road carefully at the _____

F Listen to a boy giving directions. Fill in the information. 🔊 11

How to Get to the Soccer Stadium

Best method of transportation: by (1) _____ bike _____

It takes (2) _____ minutes
and (3) _____ seconds.

Ride your bike along Park Road for
(4) _____ blocks.

Turn (5) _____ at the bookstore.

Walk through the parking lot behind the
(6) _____

Turn (7) _____ onto Apple Road.

The stadium is on the (8) _____

WHAT CAN YOU DO? Color the stars.

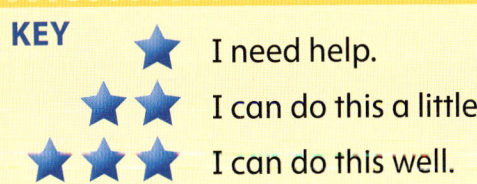

I can listen for key information
when someone gives me directions.
⭐⭐⭐

KEY	⭐	I need help.
	⭐⭐	I can do this a little.
	⭐⭐⭐	I can do this well.

Get Ready to Listen

Let's learn the **key words**.

A Read and listen to the sentences. Look up the words you don't know in your dictionary. 🔊 12

1. Go through the park. The bank is just **beyond** it.

2. Can you buy me some chocolates at the **candy store**, please?

3. Turn left. The bookstore will be the **first store on the right**.

4. **Go to the corner** and turn right.

5. The **grocery store** near my house sells fresh fish.

6. I bought a new hammer from the **hardware store**.

7. Walk **toward** the park, and call me when you are close.

8. The closest library is one block **up the street** from us.

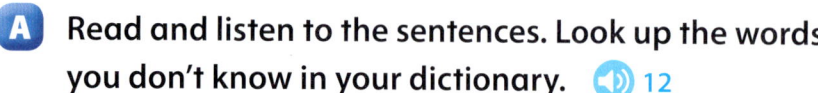

B Listen and write the number under the picture. 🔊 13

a. _____   b. __1__   c. _____   d. _____

C Read each sentence. Then listen to the words. Two of the three key words are incorrect. Write the correct key word. 🔊 14

1. This is a store that sells sweet things and chocolate.   _candy store_

2. This is a store that sells fruits and vegetables.   _____

3. This is a store that sells cans of paint and paintbrushes.   _____

4. This is the direction you go to get to something.   _____

Listen

The Cornell Method is a form of note-taking. When you take notes, write key information on the left. Write notes for the key information on the right. Then write a short summary below.

A Listen and complete the notes. 🔊 15

Key Information	Notes
1. tomatoes	
2.	1 bag, white, not brown
3. cheese	

Summary:
The woman and her son discuss the ingredients they need to make a pizza.

The Chocolate Cake

B Listen to the story *The Chocolate Cake*. What is it about? Take notes using the Cornell Method. 🔊 16

Key Information	Notes
1. eggs	
2.	
3.	

Summary:

Now read. Choose T for True or F for False.

1. Dad and Caroline have everything they need.   T   F
2. Caroline needs to go to some stores.   T   F

How many sections do you need to complete when you take **Cornell Method** notes?

WHAT CAN YOU DO?   Color the stars.

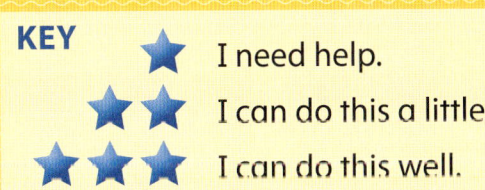

I can listen and take notes with the Cornell Method. ★★★

I can understand all of the key words. ★★★

KEY
★ I need help.
★★ I can do this a little.
★★★ I can do this well.

Understand

Remember!
When you take **Cornell Method** notes, write key information on the left and notes on the right. Then write a summary at the end.

A Think about **The Chocolate Cake**. Answer the questions and discuss with the class.

1. What words did you write in the Key Information section? Why?
2. What did you write in the Notes section? Why?
3. What did you write in the Summary section? Why?
4. Was it helpful to use the Cornell Method? Why or why not?

B Listen to **The Chocolate Cake** again. Choose **T** for **True** or **F** for **False**. 🔊 17

1. Mom's birthday is next Saturday.	T	(F)
2. Mom is going to help them make the cake.	T	F
3. Mom loves chocolate cake.	T	F
4. The grocery store is near the park.	T	F
5. They need two bars of chocolate.	T	F
6. Dad thinks that they sell cake pans at the hardware store.	T	F
7. Caroline has a cell phone.	T	F
8. Caroline thinks Dad will remember another thing they need.	T	F

C Read the sentences. Then listen to **The Chocolate Cake** again. Complete the sentences. 🔊 18

1. Caroline will have to buy a carton of _____six_____ eggs.
2. Mom's favorite chocolate is _____ chocolate.
3. The candy store is on _____ Road.
4. The hardware store is just beyond the _____

D Ask and answer the questions with a partner.

1. What stores do you go to in your town?
2. What is your favorite store and why?
3. How do you and your family celebrate birthdays?
4. If you could make your family a cake, what kind of cake would you make?

E Listen. Then read and choose the correct answer. 🔊 19

1. When the woman says *hardware store*, she means
   - ☐ a. a store that sells shoes.
   - ☐ b. a store that sells bread and cakes.
   - ☑ c. a store that sells paint and garden equipment.
   - ☐ d. a store that sells books.

2. When the boy says *candy store*, he means
   - ☐ a. a store that sells clothes.
   - ☐ b. a store that sells books.
   - ☐ c. a store that sells fruits and vegetables.
   - ☐ d. a store that sells sweet foods.

3. When the man says *up the street*, he means
   - ☐ a. along the street.
   - ☐ b. beyond the street.
   - ☐ c. toward the street.
   - ☐ d. past the street.

4. When the girl says *beyond*, she means
   - ☐ a. behind.
   - ☐ b. past.
   - ☐ c. toward.
   - ☐ d. under.

F Look and listen. Choose the best description. 🔊 20

1.
   ☐ a. ☑ b. ☐ c. ☐ d.

2.
   ☐ a. ☐ b. ☐ c. ☐ d.

3.
   ☐ a. ☐ b. ☐ c. ☐ d.

4.
   ☐ a. ☐ b. ☐ c. ☐ d.

WHAT CAN YOU DO? Color the stars.

I can use the Cornell Method to understand important information in a story. ⭐⭐⭐

KEY
⭐ I need help.
⭐⭐ I can do this a little.
⭐⭐⭐ I can do this well.

Listening Check

A Listen to the story **Treasure!** What happens? Complete the notes and choose the correct answer. 🔊 21

Key Information	Notes
1. candy store	
2.	
3.	
Summary:	

☐ a. The children find it difficult to read the treasure map.

☐ b. The children have fun following a treasure map.

B Listen to **Treasure!** again. Order the pictures. 🔊 22

a. ☐

b. ☐

c. 1

C Think about **Treasure!** and Cornell Method notes. Then choose the correct answer.

1. You hear the name of a place many times. Write it in

☐ a. Notes. ☐ b. Key Information.

2. You hear details about a place. Write them in

☐ a. Notes. ☐ b. Summary.

D Answer the questions and discuss your answers with the class.

1. What key words or phrases were repeated several times? Where did you write them?

2. What did you write for your summary? Why?

E **Listen to Treasure! again. Choose the correct answer.** 🔊 23

1. What is around the corner from the starting point?
   - ☐ a. the park
   - ☑ b. the candy store
   - ☐ c. the toy store
   - ☐ d. the bookstore

2. How do the children travel around the downtown area?
   - ☐ a. by skateboard
   - ☐ b. on foot
   - ☐ c. by bike
   - ☐ d. by bus

3. Who says they are lost?
   - ☐ a. Ayumi
   - ☐ b. Hiroto
   - ☐ c. both of them
   - ☐ d. neither of them

4. How do they feel when they find the treasure chest?
   - ☐ a. They're angry.
   - ☐ b. They're sad.
   - ☐ c. They're bored.
   - ☐ d. They think it's great.

F **Discuss with a partner.**

1. How good are you at reading a map?

2. If you could find some treasure, what would you want the treasure to be? Why?

3. Which of your friends or family would be good at reading a treasure map? Why?

G **Listen and read. Complete the sentences.** 🔊 24

I walk to school with my older brother. He walks a little too fast for me, so I have to (1) _____ hurry _____. I wish I had wheels on the bottoms of my shoes!
We walk (2) _____ the park, but we don't go through it.
We turn left just before it. We (3) _____ the bakery and the
(4) _____ and then cross the (5) _____ at the
traffic lights. Our school is (6) _____ from the intersection,
just (7) _____ the (8) _____.

WHAT CAN YOU DO? Color the stars.

I can listen for key information. ⭐⭐⭐

I can use the Cornell Method for writing notes. ⭐⭐⭐

KEY
⭐ I need help.
⭐⭐ I can do this a little.
⭐⭐⭐ I can do this well.

Get Ready to Speak

SPEAKING GOAL: Give a Speech

When you give a speech, you tell people about a subject you are interested in or know a lot about. A speech can help your audience learn or do something. It can make people laugh or cry.

A Read and listen to the speech. Underline the introduction sentence. 25

> **Speaking Tip**
> A strong introduction sentence makes people interested and want to keep listening.

My Favorite Walk

Have you ever seen a two-meter-long snake? I have, but not in a zoo. I see it on my favorite walk!

My favorite walk is a three-kilometer walk through downtown. I like it because I see, smell, and do a lot of interesting things.

The first thing I see is a snake and other jungle animals painted on the wall of our school. Every child in the school helped paint the mural last year. Then I walk past the restaurant where my mom works, and I can smell the delicious pizza! Then I go two blocks toward the park. There are a lot of pretty flowers that smell wonderful and trees that are good for climbing. Then I go back home for a family dinner. What a great walk!

B Discuss the questions with a partner.

1. How did the introduction get your attention?

2. Why is this walk the speaker's favorite walk?

3. What does he smell on his walk?

NATURAL SPEECH: Dropped Syllables

In some words, you drop (or reduce) the vowel sound in an unstressed syllable.

different	camera	vegetable
diff-rent	cam-ra	veg-ta-ble 26

Listen for **dropped syllables** in **A**. Then write down the words and cross out the dropped syllable in each. Say the words to your partner.

Speak

C Think about your favorite place to walk and what you want to say about it in a speech. Complete the diagram.

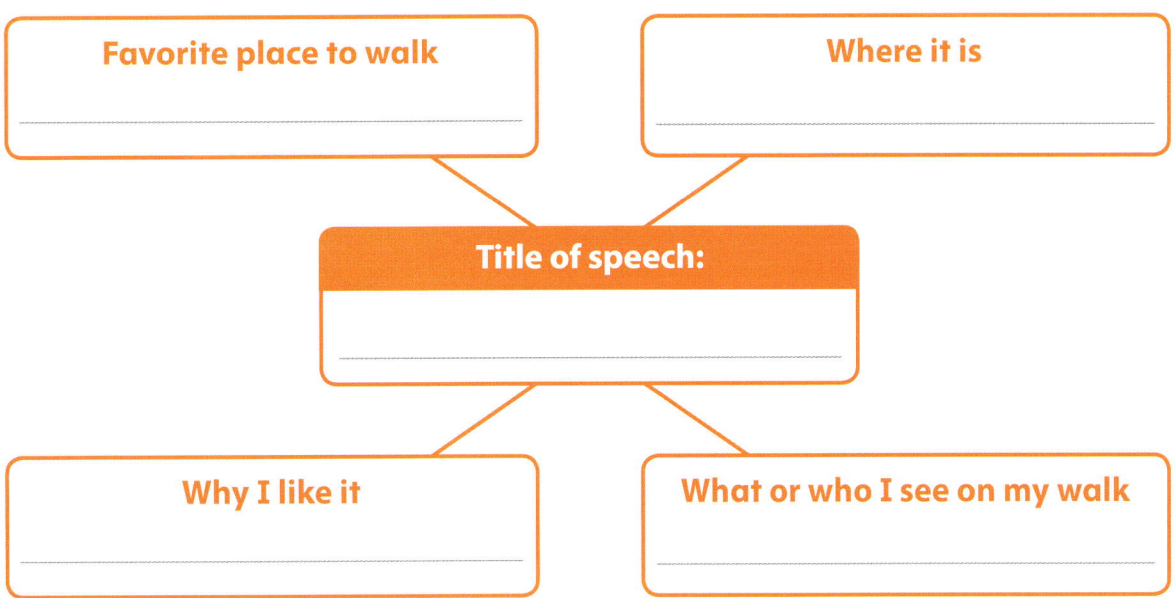

Favorite place to walk

_____

Where it is

_____

Title of speech:

_____

Why I like it

_____

What or who I see on my walk

_____

D Write about your favorite walk. Use your ideas from **C**. Choose new words, too.

1. What is your introduction sentence? Can you make it surprising or interesting?

_____

2. Where does your walk start and finish?

_____

3. What is interesting about your walk?

_____

4. Do you see, smell, or do anything interesting? Describe it.

_____

 Give your speech to the class or to a partner.

WHAT CAN YOU DO? Color the stars.

I can give a speech.
⭐⭐⭐

I can use a strong introductory sentence.
⭐⭐⭐

KEY   ⭐ I need help.
⭐⭐ I can do this a little.
⭐⭐⭐ I can do this well.

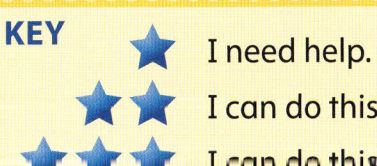

TOPIC 2

HEALTH

What Are They Like?

MY GOALS

UNIT 3

- Listen to the story *Food for the Winter*
- Listen and analyze characters

UNIT 4

- Listen to the conversation *The Broken Window*
- Listen and make value judgments

SPEAK

- Tell a fictional story

A Look at the picture.

1. What is special about these two girls?
2. Which people in your family look alike?

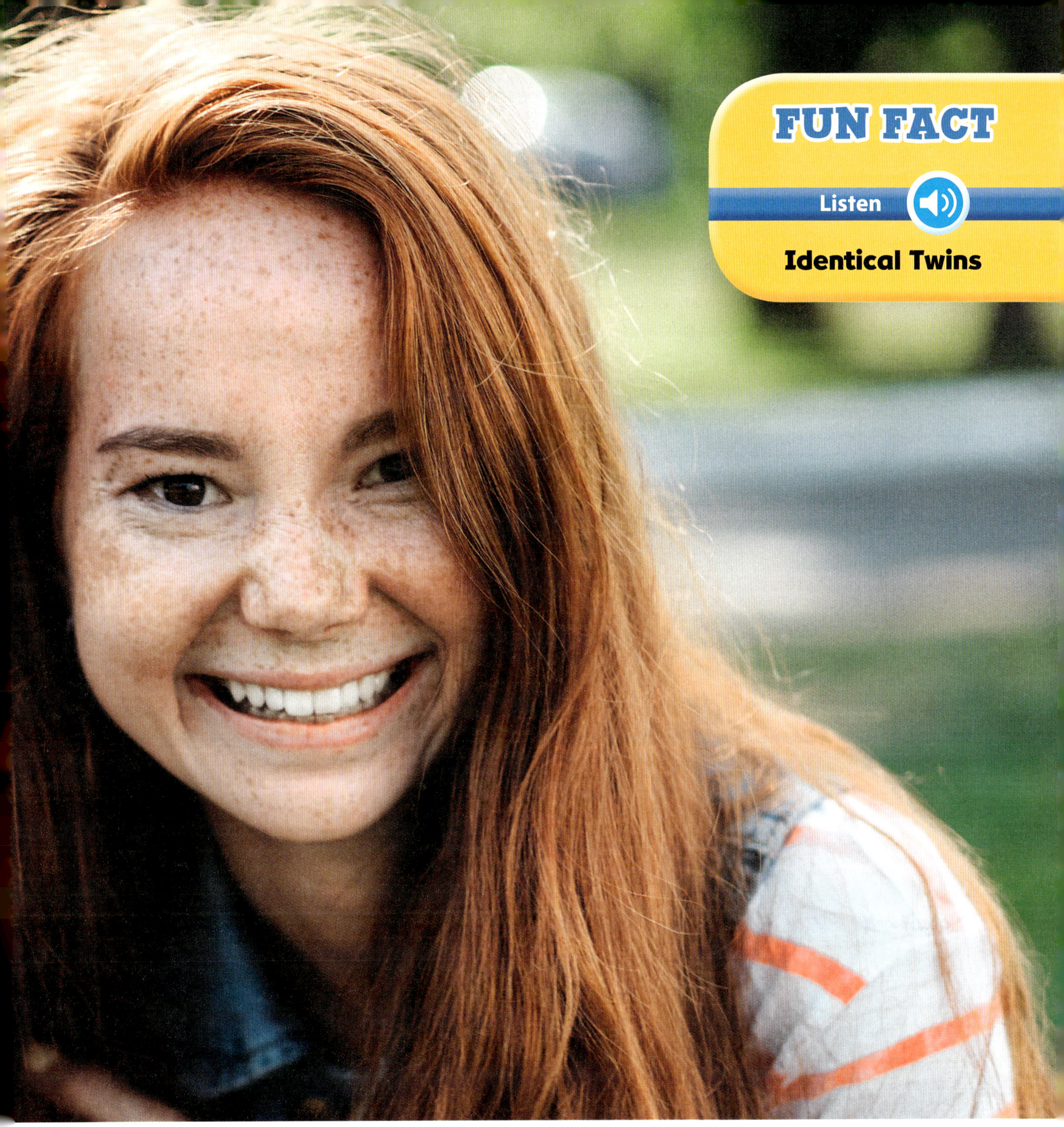

FUN FACT

Listen

Identical Twins

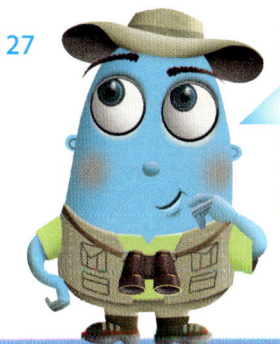

B **Listen to the Fun Fact. Then answer the questions.** 27

1. What is similar about these identical twins?
2. What is different about these identical twins?
3. How can you tell what someone's personality is like?

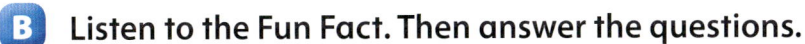

Think, Pair, Share
Would you like to be a twin? Why or why not?

Get Ready to Listen

Let's learn the **key words**.

A Read and listen to the sentences. Look up the words you don't know in your dictionary. 🔊 28

1. My mom is **cheerful** on Sundays and sings all day.
2. I'm **curious**. What's in that box? Let's open it!
3. He's **fascinated** with insects and likes watching them.
4. He was **foolish** to start his homework so late at night.
5. It's **impolite** to talk with food in your mouth.
6. It's **polite** to say *please* and *thank you*.
7. I'm always **sleepy** by 9 p.m., so I go to bed.
8. My teacher was **unhappy** about the messy classroom.

B Listen and number. 🔊 29

C Listen and complete the sentences. 🔊 30

Yesterday, I watched a TV show about dolphins. I was (1) _____!
Dolphins look like very (2) _____ animals because they often
play together. They're also very (3) _____ animals and swim
near boats to see what is happening. The show didn't finish until 10 p.m. I was very
(4) _____ by the end, so I went to bed to dream about dolphins!

Listen

LISTENING GOAL: Listen and Analyze Characters

To analyze characters, listen to what they say, what they think, what they do, how they feel, and how they look. Analyze characters to help you understand a story.

A Listen. Choose the correct answer. 🔊 31

1. ☐ a. Lisa is polite. ☐ b. Lisa is impolite.
2. ☐ a. Daniel is friendly. ☐ b. Daniel is curious.
3. ☐ a. The man is cheerful. ☐ b. The man is unhappy.

Food for the Winter

B Listen to the story *Food for the Winter*. What happens? Take notes. 🔊 32

Notes

_____

_____

_____

_____

_____

_____

Now put the sentences in order.

a. The monkey wakes up. ☐

b. The monkey can't find any food in the winter. ☐

c. The mouse asks the monkey to collect food with him. ☐

> How does **analyzing characters** help you understand the story?

WHAT CAN YOU DO? Color the stars.

I can listen and analyze characters. ⭐⭐⭐

I can understand all of the key words. ⭐⭐⭐

KEY
⭐ I need help.
⭐⭐ I can do this a little.
⭐⭐⭐ I can do this well.

Understand

Remember!
To **analyze characters**, listen carefully to what they say. Also listen for other clues about how or what they feel, think, do, and look.

A Think about **Food for the Winter**. Answer the questions and discuss with the class.

1. How do you know the monkey is impolite?
2. How do you know the monkey is foolish?
3. How do you know the monkey is unhappy?

B Listen to **Food for the Winter** again. Choose the correct answer. 🔊 33

1. What noise wakes the monkey up?
   - ☐ a. a mouse singing and dancing
   - ☐ b. a mouse taking a nap
   - ☐ c. a mouse eating berries
   - ☐ d. a mouse throwing berries into a hole

3. Five months later, the monkey is
   - ☐ a. warm and unhappy.
   - ☐ b. cheerful.
   - ☐ c. cold and cheerful.
   - ☐ d. unhappy, cold, and hungry.

2. In the summer, the monkey wants the mouse to
   - ☐ a. talk to him.
   - ☐ b. collect some food.
   - ☐ c. play with him.
   - ☐ d. take a nap.

4. At the end, the mouse wants to
   - ☐ a. share his food.
   - ☐ b. help the monkey find some food.
   - ☐ c. collect some food.
   - ☐ d. make some food.

C Read the sentences. Then listen to **Food for the Winter** again. Choose the correct answer. 🔊 34

1. The monkey takes a nap **on a rock** / **in a tree** / **under a bush**.
2. The mouse is collecting **strawberries** / **blueberries** / **blackberries**.
3. The monkey would rather **collect food** / **take a nap** / **dance and play**.
4. The monkey says the mouse is **foolish** / **impolite** / **kind**.

D Ask and answer the questions with a partner.

1. Why is it important to plan ahead?
2. Have you ever been foolish? What did you do?
3. Why is it important to work hard *and* to have fun?
4. How do you have fun in your family?

E Listen and complete the sentences. 35

sleepy	curious	fascinated	impolite	polite
	cheerful	foolish	unhappy	

1. She made a mistake and now she feels _____

2. Sandy is a really _____ man.

3. The class was _____ about their new teacher.

4. I've never been _____ at school.

5. Emma was _____ when she came home from school.

6. Lucy is always _____

7. My dad was _____ when he watched the documentary.

8. Ingrid was _____ in class.

F Listen to an e-mail. Fill in the information. 36

A Vacation E-mail

To: (1) _____ Pat

Vacation in: (2) _____

Sofia's age: (3) _____

Sofia's hair: (4) _____

Sofia's eyes: (5) _____

What Sofia is like: (6) _____ and (7) _____

Activity tomorrow: (8) _____

WHAT CAN YOU DO? Color the stars.

I can listen for what people say, do, think, feel, and look like.

KEY

 I need help.

 I can do this a little.

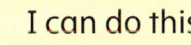 I can do this well.

Get Ready to Listen

Let's learn the **key words**.

A Read and listen to the sentences. Look up the words you don't know in your dictionary. 🔊 37

1. The **courageous** firefighter tried to put out the fire.
2. The fire in the building was big and **dangerous**.
3. I laughed all the way through the **hilarious** movie.
4. He's too **immature** to take care of his baby sister.
5. Dad's delicious tacos are always **popular** in our house.
6. It's **strange** that the door was open. I always lock it.
7. Penny was **unkind** when she took her brother's toy.
8. The people watching the fire were **worried**.

B Listen and write the number under the picture. 🔊 38

a. _____   b. _____   c. _____   d. _____

C Read each sentence. Then listen to the words. Two of the three key words are incorrect. Write the correct key word. 🔊 39

1. This is a word that means unusual. _____
2. This is how you might feel if you haven't studied for an exam. _____
3. This is a word to describe someone who is brave. _____
4. This is a word to describe someone who does things like a younger person. _____

Listen

Value judgments are opinions about what is right or wrong. When you listen, think about a character's words and actions. Ask *Did the character do the right thing? What kind of person is the character?*

A Listen and choose the correct answer. 🔊 40

1. Robert did the **right** / **wrong** thing.

2. Olivia did the **right** / **wrong** thing.

B Listen to the conversation *The Broken Window*. What happens? Take notes. 🔊 41

Notes

_____

_____

_____

_____

_____

What words and actions in the conversation help you make **value judgments**?

Now read. Choose T for True or F for False.

1. Adam was playing soccer with Nicholas and Sam.   T   F

2. Sam kicked the ball and broke the window.   T   F

3. Nicholas and Sam are still friends.   T   F

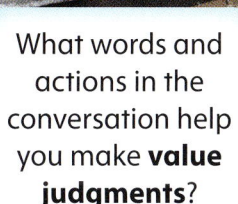

WHAT CAN YOU DO?   Color the stars.

I can listen and make value judgments.   ⭐⭐⭐

I can understand all of the key words.   ⭐⭐⭐

KEY   ⭐ I need help.

⭐⭐ I can do this a little.

⭐⭐⭐ I can do this well.

Understand

A **Think about The Broken Window. Answer the questions and discuss with the class.**

1. What is your value judgment of Nicholas's actions?
2. What is your value judgment of Sam's actions?
3. Do you have the same opinion of Nicholas from beginning to end?
4. What kind of person is Sam?

Remember! When you listen, make **value judgments** by asking *Did the character do the right thing? What kind of person is the character?*

B **Listen to The Broken Window again. Choose T for True or F for False.** 🔊 42

		T	F
1.	Adam is doing his math homework.	T	F
2.	Nicholas and Sam were playing with two boys.	T	F
3.	Nicholas kicked the ball that broke the window.	T	F
4.	No one was hurt by the broken glass.	T	F
5.	Nicholas's friends laughed about what happened.	T	F
6.	Nicholas told the truth at all times.	T	F
7.	Mom thinks Nicholas is brave for telling the truth.	T	F
8.	Nicholas and Sam played soccer again after school.	T	F

C **Read the sentences. Then listen to The Broken Window again. Complete the sentences.** 🔊 43

1. Adam and his mom were in the _____
2. The soccer ball broke the window of the _____
3. Sam had to sit outside the teacher's _____
4. After school, Nicholas and Sam played soccer in the _____

D **Ask and answer the questions with a partner.**

1. What would you do if you broke a window?
2. Have you ever done something courageous?
3. Why does it help to talk about problems with a parent?
4. What is the best way to be a good friend to someone?

E Listen. Then read and choose the correct answer. 🔊 44

1. When the boy says *strange*, he means
   ☐ a. not normal.
   ☐ b. great.
   ☐ c. perfect.
   ☐ d. pretty.

2. When the woman says *hilarious*, she means
   ☐ a. unkind.
   ☐ b. very funny.
   ☐ c. cheerful.
   ☐ d. curious.

3. When the man says *dangerous*, he means
   ☐ a. easy.
   ☐ b. difficult.
   ☐ c. not safe.
   ☐ d. interesting.

4. When the girl says *popular*, she means
   ☐ a. no one likes it.
   ☐ b. a lot of people like it.
   ☐ c. it's small.
   ☐ d. it's big.

F Look and listen. Choose the best description. 🔊 45

1.
☐ a. ☐ b. ☐ c. ☐ d.

2.
☐ a. ☐ b. ☐ c. ☐ d.

3.
☐ a. ☐ b. ☐ c. ☐ d.

4.
☐ a. ☐ b. ☐ c. ☐ d.

WHAT CAN YOU DO? Color the stars.

I can listen to a conversation and make value judgments. ★ ★ ★

KEY
★ I need help.
★ ★ I can do this a little.
★ ★ ★ I can do this well.

Listening Check

Remember!
Listen and **analyze characters**. What do they say, think, do, feel, and look like? Do they do the right thing? Make **value judgments**.

A Listen to the story **Stella the Detective!** What is it about? Take notes and choose the correct answer. 🔊 46

Notes

_____

_____

_____

_____

☐ a. Someone steals a diamond ring.

☐ b. Stella wants to find out who stole a diamond ring.

B Listen to **Stella the Detective!** again. Order the pictures. 🔊 47

a. ☐   b. ☐   c. ☐

C Think about **Stella the Detective!** Then choose the correct answer.

1. You want to understand Stella better. What do you do?

   ☐ a. analyze her words and actions   ☐ b. make a value judgment

2. You think about whether Stella is right or wrong. What are you doing?

   ☐ a. analyzing her feelings   ☐ b. making a value judgment

D Answer the questions and discuss your answers with the class.

1. What did Stella think about the young woman after watching her?

2. Was Stella's opinion about the young woman correct? How do you know?

Listen to Stella the Detective! again. Choose the correct answer. 🔊 48

1. What are some people drinking?
   - ☐ a. coffee
   - ☐ b. water
   - ☐ c. tea
   - ☐ d. milk

2. The diamond ring belongs to
   - ☐ a. the young woman.
   - ☐ b. the old lady.
   - ☐ c. Alfie.
   - ☐ d. Stella.

3. Stella found the diamond ring
   - ☐ a. near the sofa.
   - ☐ b. behind the sofa.
   - ☐ c. on the sofa.
   - ☐ d. under the sofa.

4. Alfie tells Stella that the young woman is
   - ☐ a. shy.
   - ☐ b. unkind.
   - ☐ c. foolish.
   - ☐ d. cheerful.

F **Discuss with a partner.**

1. Are you good at analyzing people? Why or why not?

2. Have you had a wrong opinion about a person? When?

3. Has anyone ever had a wrong opinion about you? What happened?

G **Listen and read. Complete the sentences.** 🔊 49

My best friend is Tim. I like him because he's always
(1) _____, even on rainy days or just before an
exam! He tells (2) _____ stories in class, and that
makes him (3) _____ with everyone. He's never
(4) _____ or (5) _____. Another good
thing about Tim is that he's (6) _____ about
everything. He always wants to learn new things. Last week I was
(7) _____ because he wanted to learn about (8) _____
snakes, but this week he wants to learn about butterflies!

WHAT CAN YOU DO? **Color the stars.**

I can analyze characters. ★ ★ ★

I can make value judgments. ★ ★ ★

KEY
★ I need help.
★ ★ I can do this a little.
★ ★ ★ I can do this well.

Get Ready to Speak

SPEAKING GOAL: Tell a Fictional Story

A fictional story is a story that you imagine. When you tell a fictional story, think about the beginning, middle, and end. Think about what your characters are like. Think about ways to make the story better and more interesting.

A **Read and listen to the story. Underline the similes and metaphors.** 50

> ### Speaking Tip
> Use similes and metaphors. A simile uses *like* or *as* to compare two different things. A metaphor compares two things that are not the same but have something in common.

The Monster in the Garden

A little girl named Pinar lived in a house with a big yard full of trees and sunshine.

Pinar loved superheroes. She liked to wear a superhero mask and a shiny cape all the time, even at bedtime!

One day, Pinar was running around the garden in the sunshine. She ran as fast as the wind. She was running so fast that she didn't see the large dark Thing in front of her, and BANG! She ran straight into it. Pinar looked up at the Thing. It was as tall as a giraffe and as big as an elephant. Pinar's legs were jelly. She couldn't run fast anymore!

"Hello, Pinar," said the Thing as it turned around. It was her dad, carrying a ladder. "I'm building you a tree house. I might need a superhero to help me."

B **Discuss the questions with a partner.**

1. What is Pinar like?
2. What is the surprise at the end of the story?
3. How do similes and metaphors make the story more interesting?

NATURAL SPEECH: Compound Nouns

A compound noun is a noun made up of two or more words (e.g., *textbook*, *video camera*). In compound nouns, the stress is usually on the first word of the compound.

Pinar wants to be a **super**hero. 51

Listen for more **compound nouns** in **A**. Say them with stress to your partner.

Speak

C Think about a fictional story you would like to tell. Complete the diagram to plan your story.

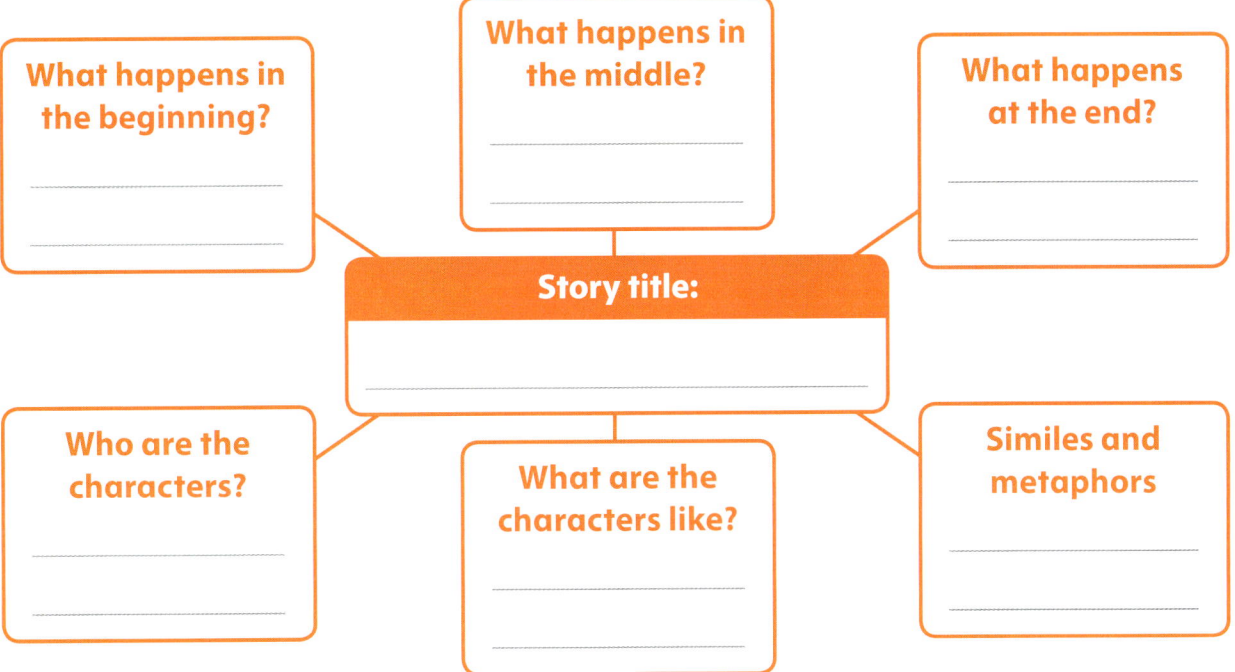

What happens in the beginning?

What happens in the middle?

What happens at the end?

Story title:

Who are the characters?

What are the characters like?

Similes and metaphors

D Write your story. Use your words from **C**. Choose new words, too.

1. How are you going to introduce your main character?

2. What is interesting about the beginning of your story?

3. What is surprising or exciting about the end of your story?

4. What are some interesting details about your characters?

 Tell your fictional story to your partner.

WHAT CAN YOU DO? Color the stars.

I can tell a fictional story. ⭐⭐⭐

I can use similes and metaphors. ⭐⭐⭐

KEY ⭐ I need help.

⭐⭐ I can do this a little.

⭐⭐⭐ I can do this well.

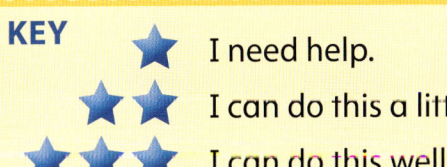

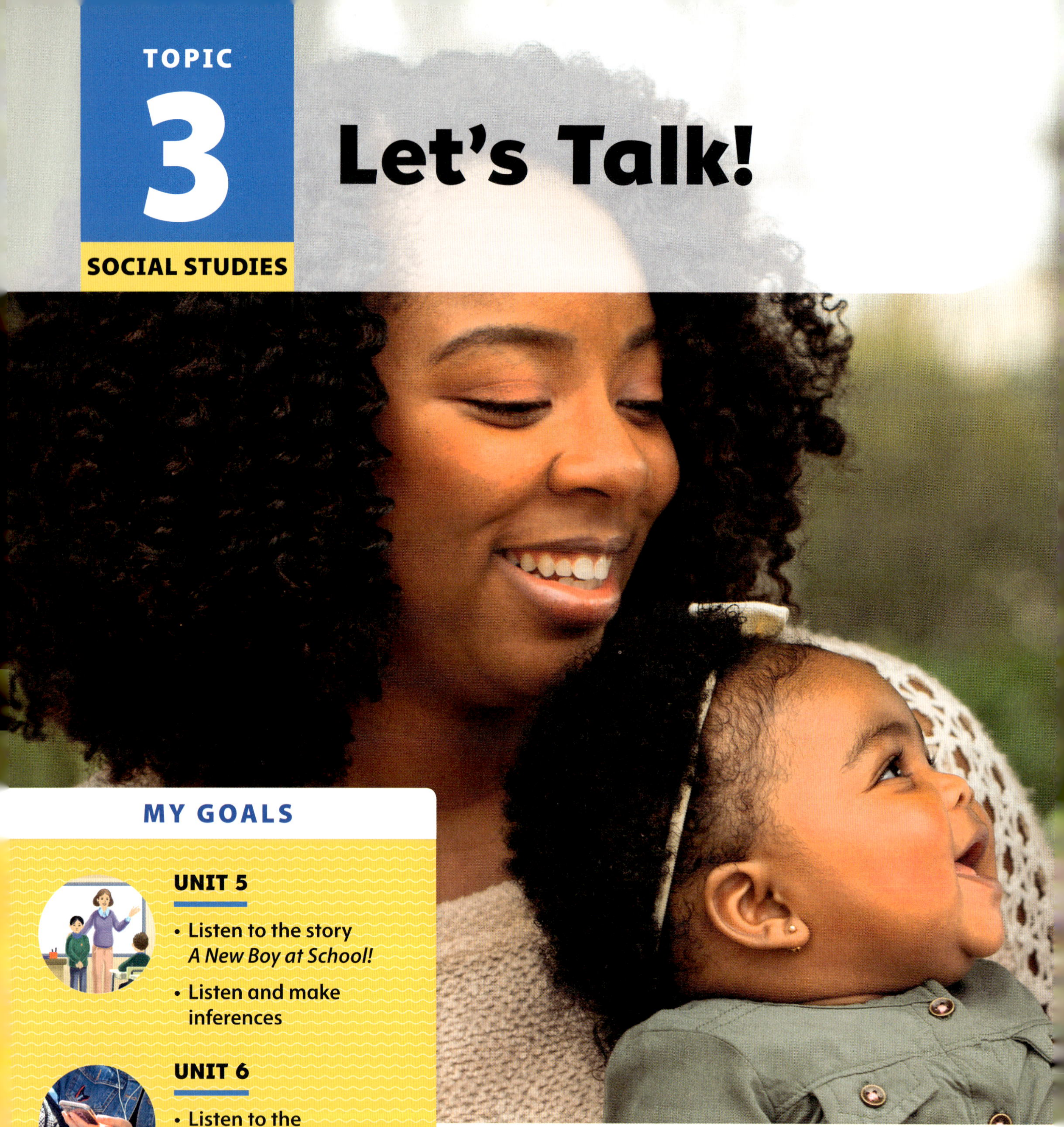

Let's Talk!

MY GOALS

UNIT 5

- Listen to the story *A New Boy at School!*
- Listen and make inferences

UNIT 6

- Listen to the conversation *Speaking Without Words*
- Listen and paraphrase

SPEAK

- Summarize

A Look at the picture.

1. What do you think the baby and dad are doing?

2. What kinds of noises have you heard a baby make?

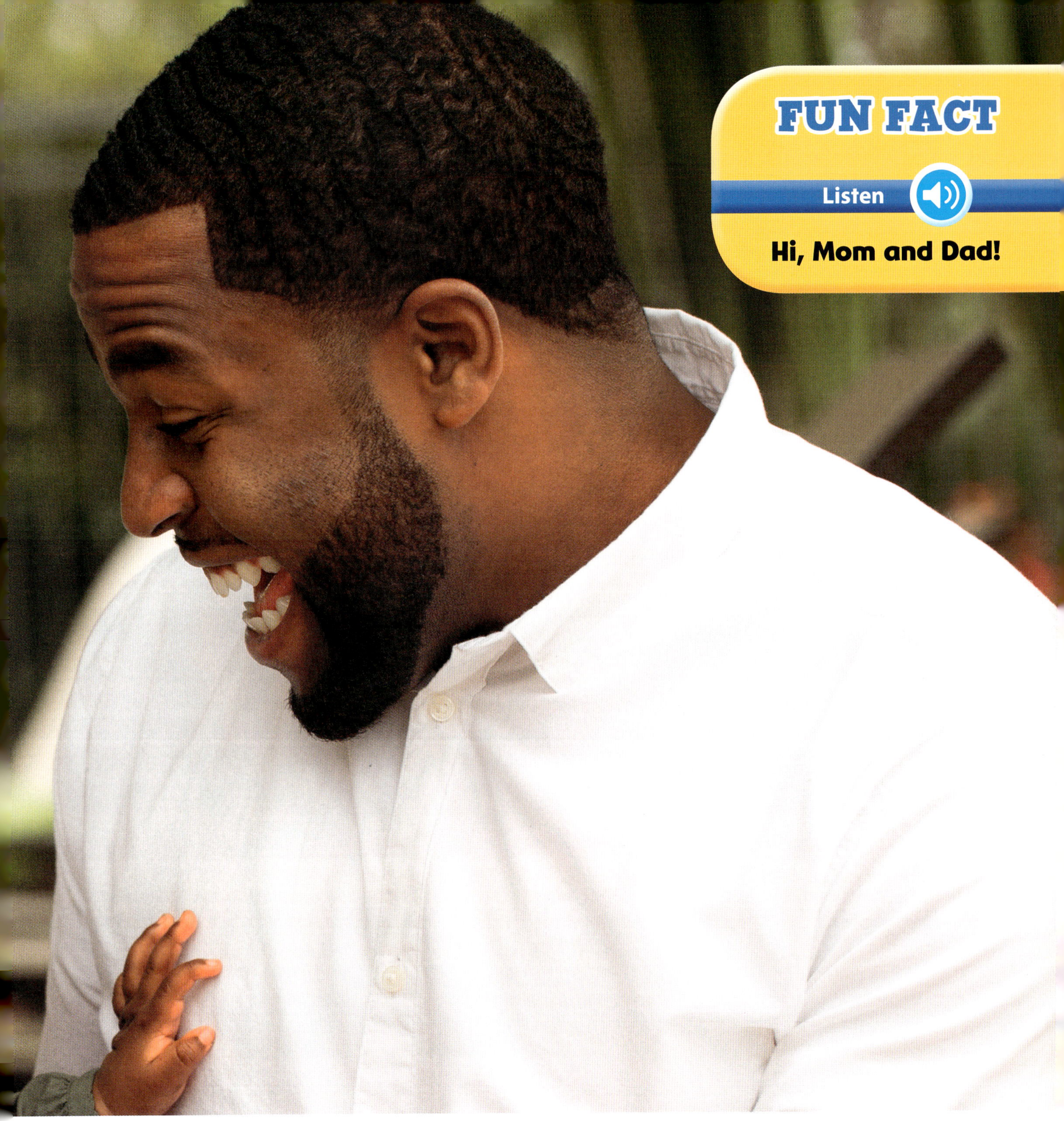

FUN FACT

Listen

Hi, Mom and Dad!

B **Listen to the Fun Fact. Then answer the questions.** 52

1. When do babies start to laugh?
2. What noises do babies make that sound like talking?
3. Why do you think babies cry?

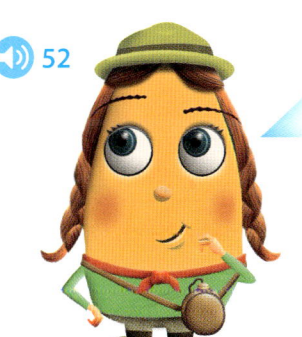

Think, Pair, Share
How do you talk to babies? What do you do differently?

Get Ready to Listen

Let's learn the **key words**.

A Read and listen to the sentences. Look up the words you don't know in your dictionary. 🔊 53

1. Alison is Canadian. She is **fluent** in English and French.
2. My **mother tongue** is the first language I spoke as a child.
3. Lucia can speak three languages. She's **multilingual**.
4. There are 11 countries in the area of **Southeast Asia**.
5. I love **Thai** food, especially the spicy shrimp soup.
6. The capital of **Thailand** is Bangkok.
7. The capital of **Vietnam** is Hanoi.
8. My friend Trang is **Vietnamese**.

Southeast Asia

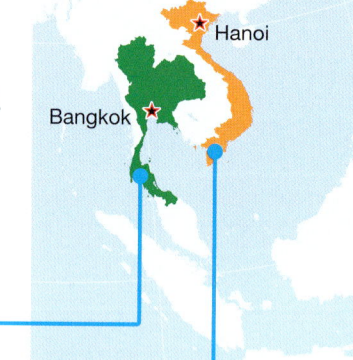

B Listen and number. 🔊 54

C Listen and complete the sentences. 🔊 55

Our teacher planned for us to have online pen pals with a class of children in Hanoi in (1) _____. I e-mail my pen pal every week. He's 11 years old, like me, and his name is Sang. He's (2) _____ in English, which is great because I don't speak any (3) _____! One day I would like to go to (4) _____ and visit Sang and his family.

Listen

LISTENING GOAL: Listen and Make Inferences

An inference is a guess about what a listening does not tell you. Use clues in the listening and what you already know to make an inference. Inferences help you understand more about a listening.

A **Listen. Choose the correct answer.** 🔊 56

1. ☐ a. Nico is nervous. ☐ b. Nico isn't nervous.
2. ☐ a. The woman likes George's hat. ☐ b. The woman wants George to buy a new hat.
3. ☐ a. Sally thinks Helena wants a cat. ☐ b. Sally doesn't know what Helena wants.

A New Boy at School!

B **Listen to the story** *A New Boy at School!* **What happens? Take notes.** 🔊 57

Notes

_____

_____

_____

_____

_____

_____

Now put the sentences in order.

a. The students ask Hien a lot of questions. ☐

b. Hien talks about his grandmother. ☐

c. Sammy buys a pineapple from the market. ☐

What clues in the story help you **make inferences**?

WHAT CAN YOU DO? Color the stars.

I can listen and make inferences. ⭐⭐⭐

I can understand all of the key words. ⭐⭐⭐

KEY

⭐ I need help.

⭐⭐ I can do this a little.

⭐⭐⭐ I can do this well.

Understand

Remember!
Listen for clues and use what you know already to **make inferences**.

A Think about **A New Boy at School!** Answer the questions and discuss with the class.

1. When Hien talks about Vietnam, how does he look and speak?

2. What can you infer about Hien?

3. What can you infer about Sammy?

B Listen to **A New Boy at School!** again. Choose the correct answer. 🔊 58

1. How many languages can Hien speak?
   - [ ] a. 2
   - [ ] b. 3
   - [ ] c. 1
   - [ ] d. 4

2. Where did Hien learn to speak English?
   - [ ] a. at school
   - [ ] b. from his friend Henri
   - [ ] c. from a book
   - [ ] d. from his parents

3. Where is Henri?
   - [ ] a. in Thailand
   - [ ] b. in Vietnam
   - [ ] c. in France
   - [ ] d. in Canada

4. What does Hien's grandmother often cook?
   - [ ] a. spicy fish
   - [ ] b. fish salad
   - [ ] c. garlic rice
   - [ ] d. fruit cake

C Read the sentences. Then listen to **A New Boy at School!** again. Choose the correct answer. 🔊 59

1. Vietnam is near **Thailand** / **France** / **Southeast Asia**.

2. Hien learned to speak **French** / **English** / **Vietnamese** first.

3. After school, Sammy goes **home** / **to the beach** / **to the market**.

4. Hien looks very **happy** / **sad** / **shy** when Sammy gives him a pineapple.

D Ask and answer the questions with a partner.

1. Have you ever been away from your home for a long time? How did you feel?

2. If a new student came to your class, how would you try to make them feel welcome?

3. How many languages can you speak? Which was the easiest to learn?

Listen and complete the sentences. 🔊 60

| Thailand | Thai | Vietnamese | Vietnam | Southeast Asia |
| fluent | multilingual | mother tongue | | |

1. Betty is going on vacation to _____

2. I can speak _____ French.

3. The flight from London to _____ was canceled.

4. You never stop learning your _____

5. The storm will hit _____ on Saturday.

6. I love _____ food.

7. For her new job, Suzy needs to be _____

8. Last week I went to an amazing _____ restaurant.

F **Listen to Vicki's travel diary. Fill in the information.** 🔊 61

Country: (1) _____

Temperature: (2) _____ degrees Celsius

Rains for: about (3) _____ minutes

Lunch yesterday: *tom yum* (4) _____

Bus trip to: (5) _____

Things to see tomorrow:

   1. the floating (6) _____

   2. the Grand (7) _____

Built in: (8) _____

WHAT CAN YOU DO? Color the stars.

I can listen for clues and use them to make inferences. ⭐⭐⭐

KEY ⭐ I need help.

⭐⭐ I can do this a little.

⭐⭐⭐ I can do this well.

UNIT 6

Get Ready to Listen

Let's learn the **key words**.

A Read and listen to the sentences. Look up the words you don't know in your dictionary. 🔊 62

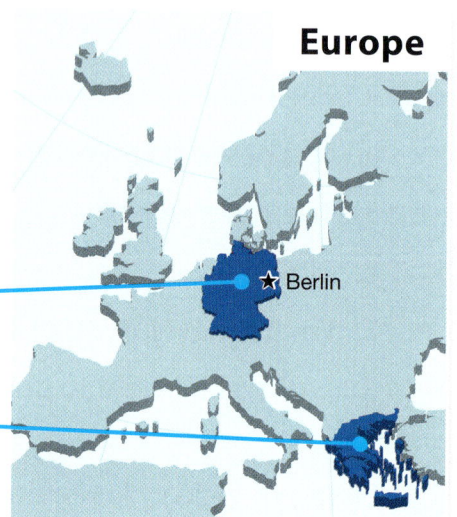

Europe

★ Berlin

1. Hans downloaded a **dictionary app** to his phone.
2. The continent of **Europe** has over 740 million people.
3. The **German** dish sauerkraut is similar to kimchi.
4. My favorite city in **Germany** is Berlin.
5. Pam made a **gesture** with her hands to tell us to be quiet.
6. There are about 6,000 islands in **Greece**!
7. My favorite food is a **Greek** salad. It's made with cheese.
8. Can you **translate** the word *hola* into English?

B Listen and write the number under the picture. 🔊 63

a. _____

b. _____

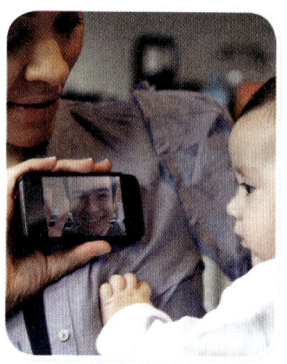
c. _____

d. _____

C Read each sentence. Then listen to the words. Two of the three key words are incorrect. Write the correct key word. 🔊 64

1. This is an area of 50 countries, including France and Italy. _____
2. This is a country next to France. _____
3. This is what you call someone from Greece. _____
4. This is what you do when you say or write the same thing in another language. _____

Listen

LISTENING GOAL: Listen and Paraphrase

Paraphrasing is putting what you hear into your own words. After you listen, paraphrase to help you understand and remember important information.

A Listen and then choose the correct paraphrase. 🔊 65

1. ☐ a. Write an essay in French about something you enjoy doing.
   ☐ b. Use a dictionary to check spelling.

2. ☐ a. Gym class is at 1 o'clock.
   ☐ b. Bring equipment. Gym class is after math.

Speaking Without Words

B Listen to the conversation *Speaking Without Words*.
What happens? Take notes. 🔊 66

Notes

_____
_____
_____
_____
_____
_____

How much information do you need to include when **paraphrasing**?

Now read. Choose T for True or F for False.

1. Renata traveled by train and ferry on her inter-railing trip.   T   F
2. Renata can speak Greek and German.   T   F
3. Renata tried different ways to speak without words.   T   F

WHAT CAN YOU DO?   Color the stars.

I can listen and paraphrase.   ★ ★ ★
I can understand all of the key words.   ★ ★ ★

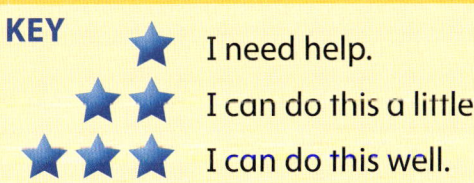

KEY
★   I need help.
★ ★   I can do this a little.
★ ★ ★   I can do this well.

Understand

Remember!
To **paraphrase**, you put what you hear into your own words.

A Think about **Speaking Without Words**. Answer the questions and discuss with the class.

1. What is Emily paraphrasing when she says, "So, it's a ticket that you can use to travel around Europe?"

2. In your own words, what does Renata say about using a dictionary app?

3. In your own words, what is speaking without words?

4. Does paraphrasing help you understand the conversation better? Why or why not?

B Listen to **Speaking Without Words** again. Choose **T** for **True** or **F** for **False**. 67

1. Renata and Emily are talking on the phone.	T	F
2. Renata went to Europe last year.	T	F
3. Emily is going to Europe next week.	T	F
4. You can use an inter-rail ticket on all trains and ferries.	T	F
5. Renata started her trip in Greece.	T	F
6. Renata suggests taking a dictionary in your bag.	T	F
7. After Germany, Renata took a train to Italy.	T	F
8. Renata is fluent in Greek.	T	F

C Read the sentences. Then listen to **Speaking Without Words** again. Complete the sentences. 🔊 68

1. Renata went inter-railing for _____ months.

2. The dictionary app was useful for reading _____ in restaurants.

3. The dictionary app was too _____ for talking to people.

4. Renata took a _____ to Greece.

D Ask and answer the questions with a partner.

1. If you could go inter-railing in Europe, which countries would you visit? Why?

2. Have you ever tried speaking to someone without words? What happened?

3. What gestures could you use to buy a bottle of water?

E Listen. Then read and choose the correct answer. 🔊 69

1. When the woman says *gesture*, she means
   - ☐ a. an action with her hands.
   - ☐ b. a dictionary.
   - ☐ c. a dictionary app.
   - ☐ d. a guess.

2. When the girl says *German*, she means
   - ☐ a. a person from China.
   - ☐ b. a person from Greece.
   - ☐ c. a person from France.
   - ☐ d. a person from Germany.

3. When the man says *dictionary app*, he means
   - ☐ a. a software program.
   - ☐ b. a textbook.
   - ☐ c. an online game.
   - ☐ d. a new phone.

4. When the boy says *Greece*, he means
   - ☐ a. a country in Southeast Europe.
   - ☐ b. a country in Southeast Asia.
   - ☐ c. a country in South America.
   - ☐ d. a country in Northern Europe.

F Look and listen. Choose the best description. 🔊 70

1.

☐ a. ☐ b. ☐ c. ☐ d.

2.

☐ a. ☐ b. ☐ c. ☐ d.

3.

☐ a. ☐ b. ☐ c. ☐ d.

4.

☐ a. ☐ b. ☐ c. ☐ d.

WHAT CAN YOU DO? Color the stars.

I can paraphrase to understand and remember important information.
⭐⭐⭐

KEY
⭐ I need help.
⭐⭐ I can do this a little.
⭐⭐⭐ I can do this well.

Remember!
Listen carefully for clues to **make inferences**, and then put what you hear in your own words to **paraphrase**.

A Listen to the TV interview **A New Life**. What is it about? Take notes and choose the correct answer. 🔊 71

Notes

_____

_____

_____

_____

☐ a. Elliot and Niran ate a pizza together.

☐ b. Elliot and Niran became friends without speaking each other's language.

B Listen to **A New Life** again. Order the pictures. 🔊 72

a. ☐

b. ☐

c. ☐

C Think about **A New Life**. Then choose the correct answer.

1. You want to know how Elliot feels. What should you do?

    ☐ a. make inferences   ☐ b. paraphrase

2. You want to remember the important things from the passage. What should you do?

    ☐ a. make inferences   ☐ b. paraphrase

D Answer the questions and discuss your answers with the class.

1. How does Elliot feel about his new life in Thailand? What clues did you use to infer how he feels?

2. How can you paraphrase what Elliot and Niran did when they first met?

E Listen to **A New Life** again. Choose the correct answer. 🔊 73

1. Where is Chang Mai?

☐ a. in Vietnam
☐ b. in Thailand
☐ c. in Europe
☐ d. in the UK

2. What did the boys drink?

☐ a. milk
☐ b. water
☐ c. soda
☐ d. juice

3. Which three words are the same in English and Thai?

☐ a. pizza, computer, TV
☐ b. juice, gesture, pizza
☐ c. pizza, cartoon, dictionary
☐ d. pizza, soccer, park

4. Can Elliot speak Thai now?

☐ a. No, because he doesn't want to learn Thai.
☐ b. He can only speak three words in Thai.
☐ c. Yes, but he's not fluent.
☐ d. Yes, and he's fluent.

F Discuss with a partner.

1. Why do you think Elliot and Niran become best friends?

2. How would you feel if you moved to a new country and you didn't speak the language?

3. How would you make friends with someone who speaks a different language?

G Listen and read. Complete the sentences. 🔊 74

Welcome back to Sports Radio. I'm at the Olympic stadium, watching the 100-meter race. There are three runners in the race. On the left is Hom Na from (1) _____, in (2) _____, and then two runners from (3) _____ — Agnes Callas from (4) _____ and Hannah Weber from (5) _____. And the race has begun! The (6) _____ runner is in front, but ... oh, wait. Now the (7) _____ runner has moved to the front. They are very close. And here comes the (8) _____ runner, moving as fast as she can. Excellent work. And it's Greece first, Thailand second, and Germany third.

WHAT CAN YOU DO? Color the stars.

I can listen and make inferences. ⭐⭐⭐

I can listen and paraphrase. ⭐⭐⭐

KEY ⭐ I need help.

⭐⭐ I can do this a little.

⭐⭐⭐ I can do this well.

Get Ready to Speak

SPEAKING GOAL: Summarize

When you summarize, think about the main ideas in a passage and say what the passage is about in a few sentences.

A Read and listen to the text. Then read and listen to the summary. Underline the main ideas. 75

> **Speaking Tip**
> When you summarize, include main ideas but not the details of a passage.

How to Remember New Words

There are so many words in a language that we have to remember, and it can be difficult. How can we try to remember them?

There are lots of different ways. My favorite is to write the word in a notebook and draw a little picture next to it. Then, when I am trying to remember the word, I see the picture in my head and it helps me to remember it. Another good way is to write a sentence using the word. So, for example, for the word *month*, you could write, *month: My birthday is in the month of June.*

Summary

You can draw pictures of new words and write new words in sentences to help remember them.

B Discuss the questions with a partner.

1. What is the writer's favorite way to remember words?

2. Does the title give the same information as the summary? Why or why not?

3. How would you summarize the text in your own words?

 NATURAL SPEECH: *Have To*

In conversations, words can sound different from how they are written. The verb *have to* can sound like *hafta*.

See you, Lisa. I have to be home by 6:00 p.m. 76

Listen to **have to** in **A**. Then write three sentences using **have to**. Say them with your partner.

Speak

C Think of a movie or book in a different language or from a different place. Summarize the main ideas of the story and complete the diagram.

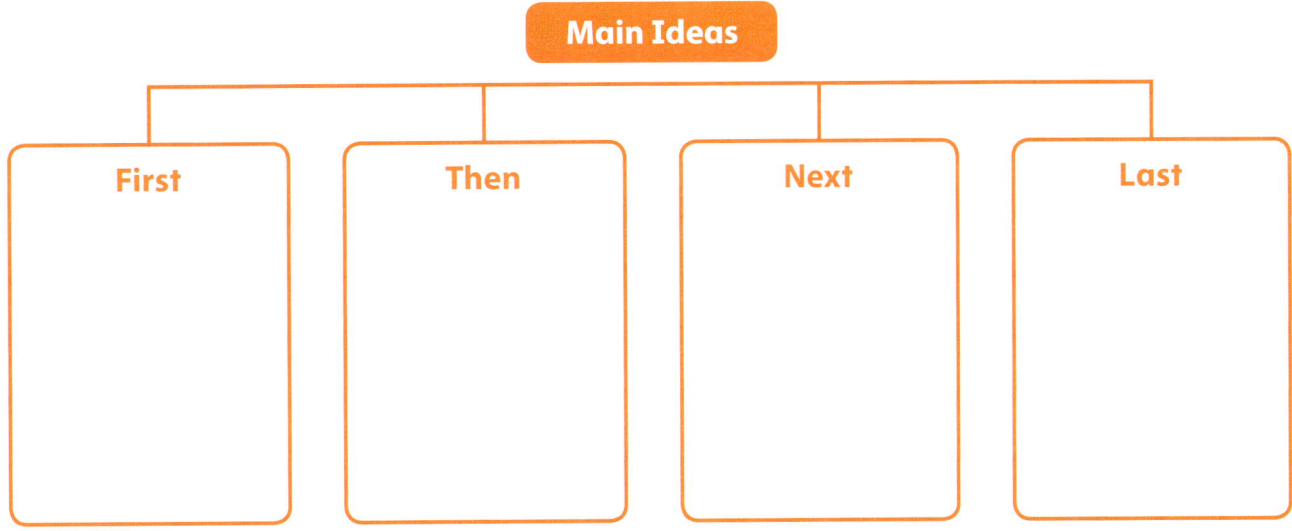

Main Ideas

First	Then	Next	Last

D Write a summary of the movie or book. Use your words from **C**. Choose new words, too.

1. Who are the main characters in the movie or book?

   _____

2. What happens first?

   _____

3. What happens next?

   _____

4. How does the story end?

   _____

 Tell your summary to the class or a partner.

WHAT CAN YOU DO?   Color the stars.

I can summarize.
⭐⭐⭐

I can avoid using details in my summary.
⭐⭐⭐

KEY   ⭐ I need help.

⭐⭐ I can do this a little.

⭐⭐⭐ I can do this well.

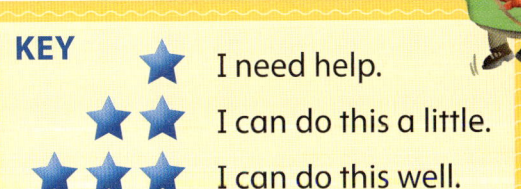

4

GEOGRAPHY

Fun in the Sun

MY GOALS

UNIT 7

- Listen to the story *A Family Vacation*
- Listen for the speaker's purpose

UNIT 8

- Listen to the conversation *Airport Adventures*
- Listen for advice

SPEAK

- Give advice

 Look at the picture.

1. What do you see? Do you want to go there? Why or why not?

2. Where do you think this is? Why?

FUN FACT

Listen 🔊

A Lot of Water!

B Listen to the Fun Fact. Then answer the questions. 🔊 77

1. Where is Iguazu Falls?

2. How high are some of the waterfalls?

3. Would you like to visit Iguazu Falls?
   Why or why not?

Think, Pair, Share
Imagine you are visiting Iguazu Falls. What can you hear, feel, and smell?

Get Ready to Listen

Let's learn the **key words**.

A **Read and listen to the sentences. Look up the words you don't know in your dictionary.** 🔊 78

1. Lucia will **go bungee jumping** from a bridge.
2. When you **go caving**, you need a helmet with a light on it.
3. Anthony wants to **go rafting** on the river.
4. Let's **go scuba diving** to see the fish and turtles.
5. I can't **go skydiving**. I'm afraid to jump out of a plane.
6. When you go rock climbing, you have to wear a **harness**.
7. I went to an amusement park to **ride a roller coaster**.
8. Cameron held on to the **rope** as he climbed.

B **Listen and number.** 🔊 79

C **Listen and complete the sentences.** 🔊 80

In the summer, I went to an activity camp in China. I went (1) _____
for the first time and I saw bats. I didn't go (2) _____, because I was
scared, but I did go surfing and (3) _____. I rode a horse and went
hiking in the mountains. And on the last day I went to a theme park and rode the highest
(4) _____ in China. I loved it!

Listen

LISTENING GOAL: Listen for the Speaker's Purpose

A speaker has a purpose, or reason, for speaking. That purpose can be to give information. It can also be to make you believe or enjoy something. When you listen, ask *Who is speaking?* and *Why is the speaker saying this?*

A Listen. Choose the correct answer. 🔊 81

1. The teacher's purpose is to
   - ☐ a. give information to the students.
   - ☐ b. make the students laugh.

2. The girl's purpose is to
   - ☐ a. let Luka know she's sorry.
   - ☐ b. tell Luka his radio is broken.

B Listen to the story *A Family Vacation*. What happens? Take notes. 🔊 82

A Family Vacation

Notes

_____

_____

_____

_____

Now put the sentences in order.

a. The travel agent suggests a hiking trip through the Amazon jungle. ☐

b. The family tells the travel agent that they want a vacation. ☐

c. The son suggests that they stay at home for their vacation. ☐

What's the **purpose** of the family's visit to the travel agency?

WHAT CAN YOU DO? Color the stars.

I can listen for the speaker's purpose. ⭐⭐⭐

I can understand all of the key words. ⭐⭐⭐

KEY

⭐ I need help.

⭐⭐ I can do this a little.

⭐⭐⭐ I can do this well.

Understand

Remember!
The speaker's **purpose** may be to give information, make you believe something, or make you enjoy something.

A Think about **A Family Vacation**. Answer the questions and discuss with the class.

1. What different purposes does the travel agent have when talking to the family?

2. What is the reason the daughter speaks?

3. What is the reason the son speaks?

B Listen to **A Family Vacation** again. Choose the correct answer. 🔊 83

1. The family wants to go on vacation in
   - ☐ a. June.
   - ☐ b. July.
   - ☐ c. August.
   - ☐ d. September.

2. Where does the travel agent say they can go rafting?
   - ☐ a. Australia
   - ☐ b. Brazil
   - ☐ c. Mexico
   - ☐ d. California

3. What can they do in the Amazon jungle?
   - ☐ a. go scuba diving
   - ☐ b. go rafting
   - ☐ c. go hiking
   - ☐ d. go caving

4. Who is scared of spiders?
   - ☐ a. Mom
   - ☐ b. Dad
   - ☐ c. Alicia
   - ☐ d. William

C Read the sentences. Then listen to **A Family Vacation** again. Choose the correct answer. 🔊 84

1. At the Grand Canyon you can **go skydiving** / **go bungee jumping** / **ride a roller coaster**.

2. The travel agent suggests going caving in **Australia** / **Mexico** / **Brazil**.

3. Mom is scared of **being up high** / **swimming** / **the dark**.

4. The son wants to **go scuba diving** / **ride his bike** / **go rafting**.

D Ask and answer the questions with a partner.

1. What are you scared of?

2. If you could go on a trip, where would you go and what would you do?

3. Why do people like adventure sports such as scuba diving, skydiving, and rafting?

E Listen and complete the sentences. 🔊 85

| caving | rafting | go skydiving | go bungee jumping |
| rope | harness | go scuba diving | ride a roller coaster |

1. The _____ keeps you safe when you're rock climbing.

2. I'm too scared to _____

3. I've always wanted to go _____

4. Ben is going to _____ on his vacation.

5. Always check the _____ before you climb.

6. Are you brave enough to _____

7. Egypt and Turkey are good places to _____

8. Sara went _____ on her vacation to Turkey.

F Listen to the travel brochure. Fill in the information. 🔊 86

Sport: (1) _____

Lowest age: (2) _____

At 15 you can dive to (3) _____ meters.

Swimming test: swim for (4) _____ meters, stay in water for

(5) _____ minutes

The classes take (6) _____ days.

Practice in a (7) _____ or the sea.

WHAT CAN YOU DO? Color the stars.

I can listen for the speaker's purpose.
⭐⭐⭐

KEY
⭐ I need help.
⭐⭐ I can do this a little.
⭐⭐⭐ I can do this well.

Get Ready to Listen

Let's learn the **key words**.

A Read and listen to the sentences. Look up the words you don't know in your dictionary. 🔊 87

1. Your seat number is printed on your **boarding pass**.
2. Anna's **carry-on luggage** is a backpack.
3. She dropped off her suitcase at **check-in**.
4. Jin-Tae is late. His flight is **delayed** by two hours.
5. I will **exchange** my US dollars for Canadian dollars.
6. Ben is happy because his flight left **on time**.
7. You must have your **passport** to travel to another country.
8. We need to open our bags at **security**.

B Listen and write the number under the picture. 🔊 88

a. _____

b. _____

c. _____

d. _____

C Read each sentence. Then listen. Two of the three key words are incorrect. Write the correct key word. 🔊 89

1. This is where you drop off your suitcase. _____
2. This is a piece of paper with your seat number on it. _____
3. This important item has your photo, name, and birthday. _____
4. This is what you say when a 3 p.m. flight leaves at 3 p.m. _____

Listen

LISTENING GOAL: Listen for Advice

Advice is an opinion about what a person should do. Listen for *should* to identify the advice someone gives.

A **Listen and choose the advice.** 🔊 90

1. ☐ a. Go to the new café.
   ☐ b. Have the lemon cake.
   ☐ c. It's delicious.

2. ☐ a. Stay calm.
   ☐ b. Learn some safety rules.
   ☐ c. Fall out of the boat.

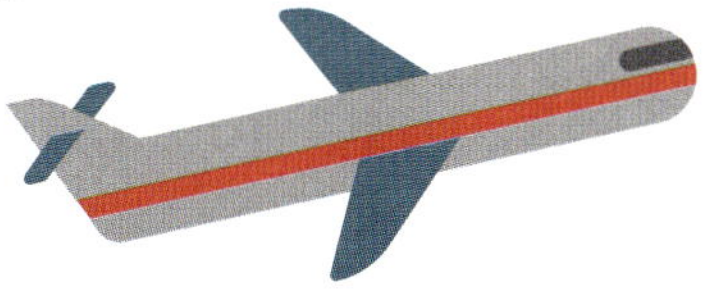

Airport Adventures

B **Listen to the conversation *Airport Adventures*.
What is it about? Take notes.** 🔊 91

Notes

_____

_____

_____

_____

_____

_____

Now read. Choose T for True or F for False.

1. Uncle Richard explains what to do when you get to the airport. **T F**

2. Uncle Richard describes his trip to Singapore. **T F**

3. Uncle Richard describes his job at the airport. **T F**

What is Uncle Richard's first piece of **advice**?

WHAT CAN YOU DO? Color the stars.

I can listen for advice. ⭐⭐⭐

I can understand all of the key words. ⭐⭐⭐

KEY

⭐ I need help.

⭐⭐ I can do this a little.

⭐⭐⭐ I can do this well.

Understand

Remember!
Use *should* when giving **advice**.

A Think about **Airport Adventures**. Answer the questions and discuss with the class.

1. How does Julian ask for advice?
2. What do you think is Uncle Richard's most interesting advice?
3. What should Julian do before he goes to the airport?
4. What advice does Uncle Richard give Julian about the waiting area?

B Listen to **Airport Adventures** again. Choose **T** for **True** or **F** for **False**. 92

1. Uncle Richard is flying to Singapore next week.   T   F
2. Julian has never traveled by plane before.   T   F
3. You can download your boarding pass onto your phone.   T   F
4. You can't take any bags on the plane.   T   F
5. After check-in you go to security.   T   F
6. Most flights are delayed.   T   F
7. You should exchange your money when you arrive.   T   F
8. A bank will exchange your money.   T   F

C Read the sentences. Then listen to **Airport Adventures** again. Complete the sentences. 93

1. The airline e-mails your _____
2. You should arrive at the airport _____ hours before your flight leaves.
3. Your carry-on luggage should be a _____ bag.
4. After security, go through to the _____

D Ask and answer the questions with a partner.

1. Have you traveled by plane or do you want to? Why or why not?
2. If you could fly anywhere, where would you go and why?
3. Would you like to be a pilot? Why or why not?

E Listen. Then read and choose the correct answer. 🔊 94

1. When the woman says *carry-on luggage*, she means
   - ☐ a. a large suitcase.
   - ☐ b. a box.
   - ☐ c. a small bag.
   - ☐ d. a pencil case.

2. When the boy says *security*, he means
   - ☐ a. an area where you can drop off your suitcase.
   - ☐ b. an area where you can watch the planes.
   - ☐ c. an area where you show your passport.
   - ☐ d. an area where you can buy food and drinks.

3. When the man says *delayed*, he means
   - ☐ a. his flight is late.
   - ☐ b. his flight is early.
   - ☐ c. his flight is empty.
   - ☐ d. his flight is full.

4. When the girl says *exchange*, she means
   - ☐ a. change her money to a different country's money.
   - ☐ b. give money.
   - ☐ c. lose money.
   - ☐ d. take her money to a different country.

F Look and listen. Choose the best description. 🔊 95

1.

☐ a. ☐ b. ☐ c. ☐ d.

2.

☐ a. ☐ b. ☐ c. ☐ d.

3.

☐ a. ☐ b. ☐ c. ☐ d.

4.

☐ a. ☐ b. ☐ c. ☐ d.

WHAT CAN YOU DO?   Color the stars.

I can listen for advice in a conversation about traveling.
★★★

KEY
★ I need help.
★★ I can do this a little.
★★★ I can do this well.

Listening Check

> **Remember!**
> Listen carefully to understand the speaker's **purpose**. Who is speaking and why? Listen for *should* to identify **advice**.

A Listen to the report **A Perfect Day in Turkey**. What is it about? Take notes and choose the correct answer. 🔊 96

Notes

_____

_____

_____

_____

_____

- [ ] a. Zeynep is giving advice and information about visiting Cappadocia.
- [ ] b. Zeynep wants to sell you a vacation to Cappadocia.

B Listen to **A Perfect Day in Turkey** again. Order the pictures. 🔊 97

a.
[ ]

b.
[ ]

c.
[ ]

C Think about **A Perfect Day in Turkey**. Then choose the correct answer.

1. You want to know what to do in Cappadocia. What should you do?
   - [ ] a. listen for purpose
   - [ ] b. listen for advice

2. You want to know why Zeynep is telling you about Cappadocia. What should you do?
   - [ ] a. listen for purpose
   - [ ] b. listen for advice

D Answer the questions and discuss your answers with the class.

1. In your opinion, what is Zeynep's most useful advice?

2. Is Zeynep a good person to give advice about Cappadocia? Why or why not?

E Listen to **A Perfect Day in Turkey** again. Choose the correct answer. 🔊 98

1. Where in Turkey is Cappadocia?
   - ☐ a. in the west
   - ☐ b. in the east
   - ☐ c. in the center
   - ☐ d. in the north

2. When should you take a hot-air-balloon ride?
   - ☐ a. in the morning
   - ☐ b. in the afternoon
   - ☐ c. in the evening
   - ☐ d. at night

3. How many doors are there to the underground city?
   - ☐ a. 12
   - ☐ b. 20,000
   - ☐ c. 50
   - ☐ d. 600

4. What money do they use in Turkey?
   - ☐ a. baht
   - ☐ b. rupee
   - ☐ c. lira
   - ☐ d. dollar

F Discuss with a partner.

1. Would you do any of the activities Zeynep suggests? Which ones?
2. What activities could a visitor do around your town?
3. What advice would you give to someone visiting and traveling around your country?

G Listen and read. Complete the sentences. 🔊 99

On our trip to Brazil, we were nearly late for the flight because Dad couldn't find his (1) _____. But then I found it in his (2) _____, right before (3) _____ was closing. Then he couldn't find our (4) _____, but I remembered that they were downloaded onto his phone! Luckily, our flight was (5) _____ by 30 minutes, so we still got on the plane. When we arrived, we wanted to (6) _____. We each put on a (7) _____ and checked the (8) _____, but then we decided it was too scary!

WHAT CAN YOU DO? Color the stars.

I can listen for the speaker's purpose.
⭐⭐⭐

I can listen for advice.
⭐⭐⭐

KEY
⭐ I need help.
⭐⭐ I can do this a little.
⭐⭐⭐ I can do this well.

Get Ready to Speak

SPEAKING GOAL: Give Advice

When you give advice, you tell what someone should do or how they should do it. Use your own experiences and your opinions.

A Read and listen to the advice. Underline *should*.  100

> **Speaking Tip**
> Use *should* when you give advice.

Gauja National Park

If you come to Latvia for a vacation, you should visit Gauja National Park. It's the largest park in Latvia, and there are lots of fun activities you can do in the park. In the winter, you can go skiing — there's always a lot of snow!

In the spring and summer, you can go cycling or hiking. But my favorite thing to do is go caving. There are lots of different caves, and they're all amazing. But you should always be safe and only go into the caves with a guide.

But I think the best time to visit is in the fall, when the leaves on the trees are turning orange and red. Then I think it's the most beautiful place in the world!

B Discuss the questions with a partner.

1. What is the speaker's advice for an activity in Latvia?

2. What advice does the speaker give about staying safe?

3. Does the speaker's advice make you want to visit Gauja National Park? Why or why not?

 NATURAL SPEECH: Syllable Stress

In words with two or more syllables, you usually stress one syllable.

Latvia

va**ca**tion 🔊 101

Listen for **syllable stress** in **A**. Underline the stressed syllables in the words *national, activities, winter,* and *amazing*. Say them with stress to your partner.

Speak

C Think about a place you know. What advice would you give about visiting the place? Complete the diagram.

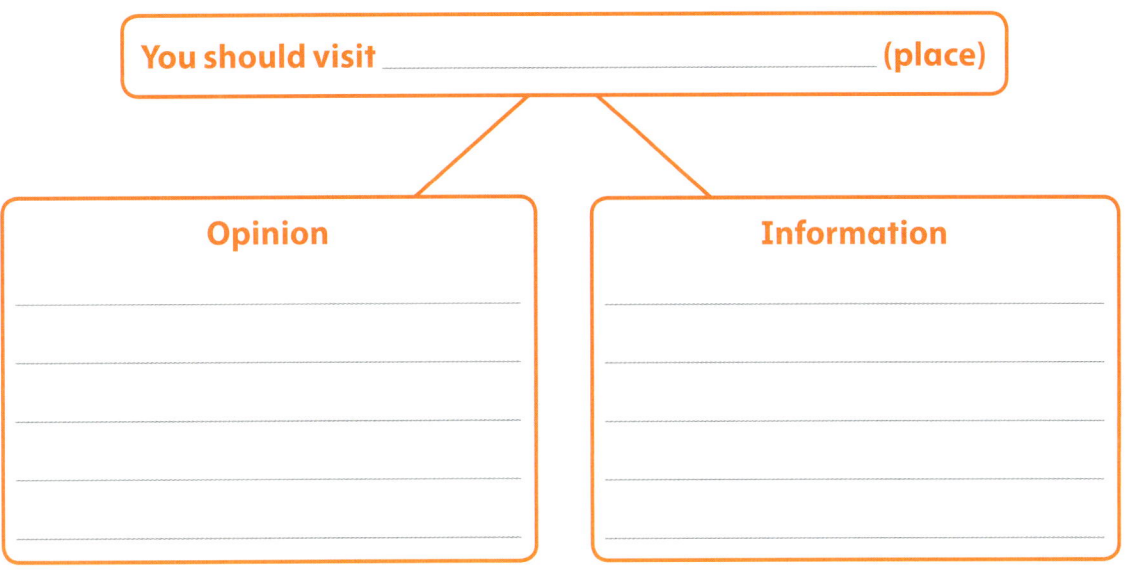

You should visit _____ (place)

Opinion	Information

D Write your advice. Use your words from **C**. Choose new words, too.

1. Where should people go?

   _____

2. Why should they go there?

   _____

3. What should they do there?

   _____

4. What shouldn't they do there?

   _____

 With a partner, talk about your place and your advice.

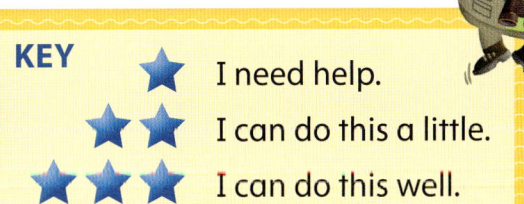

WHAT CAN YOU DO? Color the stars.

I can give advice. ★★★

I can use *should*. ★★★

KEY

★ I need help.

★★ I can do this a little.

★★★ I can do this well.

Our Beautiful Planet

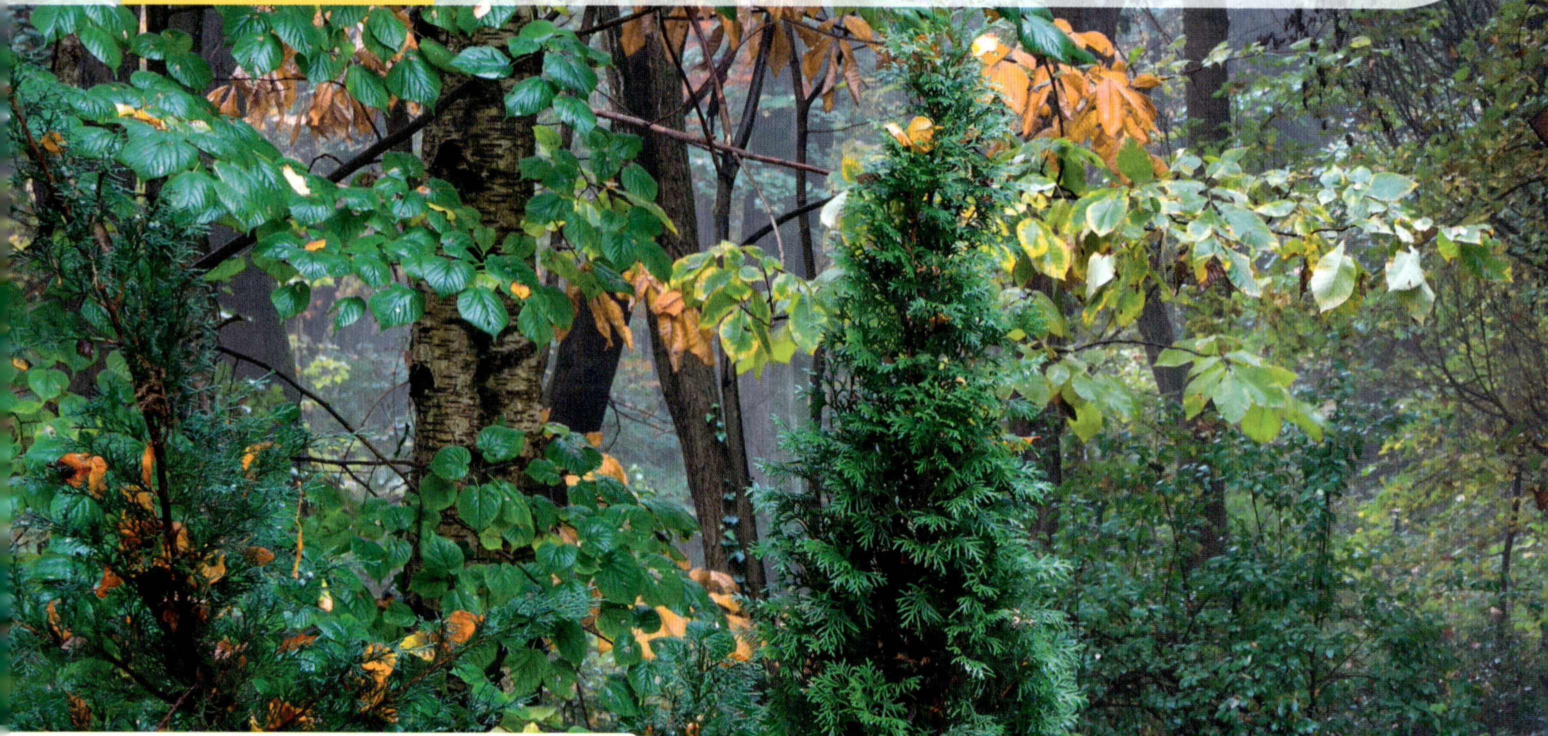

MY GOALS

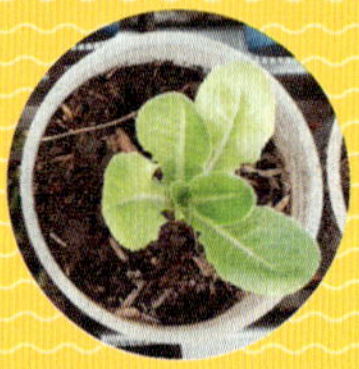

UNIT 9

- Listen to the letter *The Three Rs*
- Listen for complaints

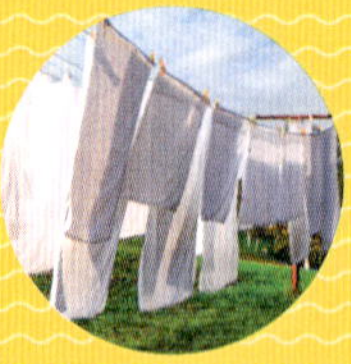

UNIT 10

- Listen to the interview *How Do You Help?*
- Listen for reasons

SPEAK

- Make an apology

A Look at the picture.

1. What do you think this is?
2. What do you think it might be used for?

FUN FACT

Listen

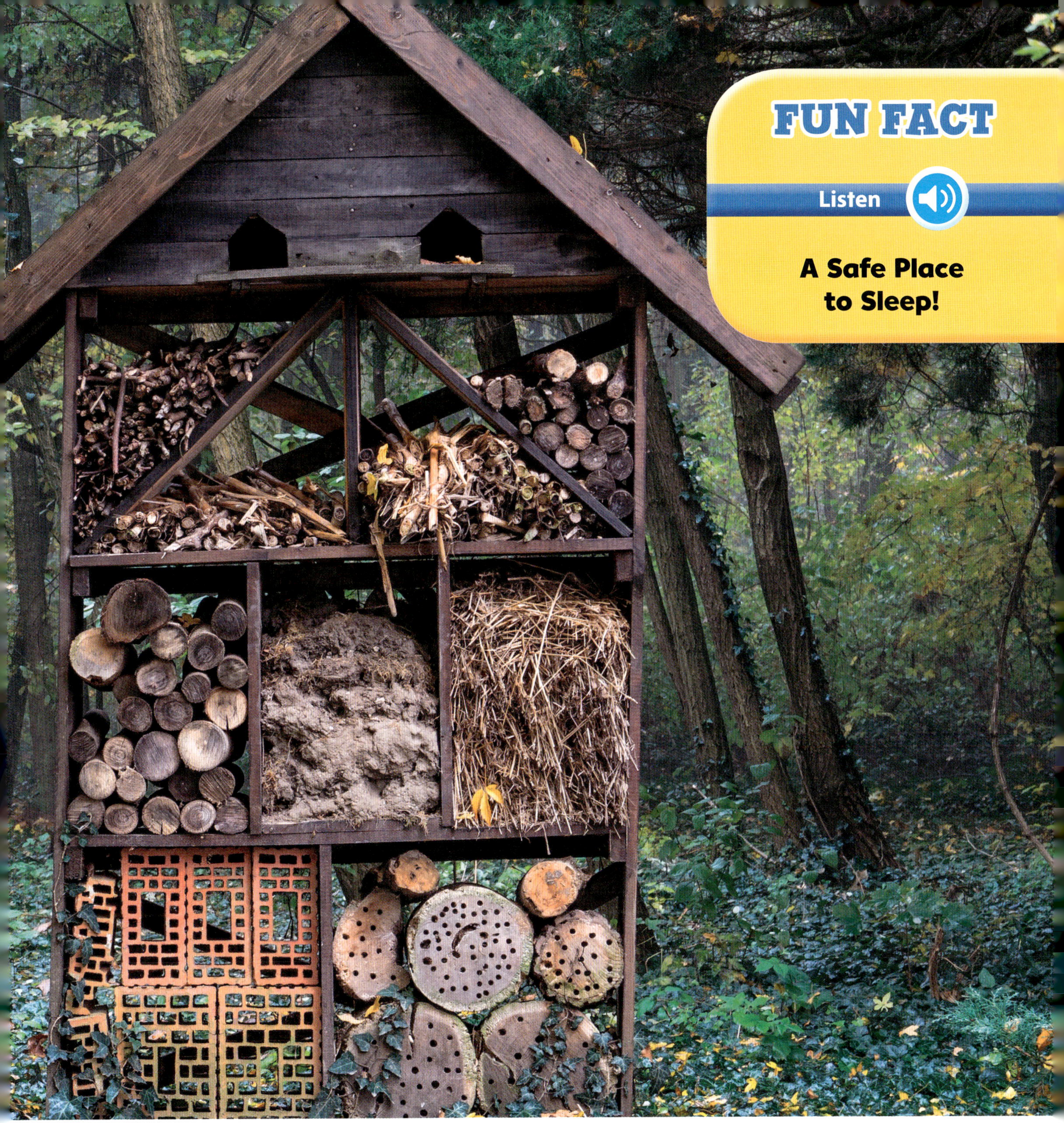

A Safe Place to Sleep!

B **Listen to the Fun Fact. Then answer the questions.** 102

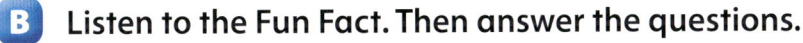

1. Where do bees like to sleep?
2. Where do ladybugs like to sleep?
3. Would you like to make a bug hotel? Why or why not?

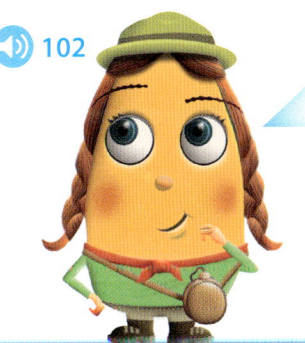

Think, Pair, Share
Do you like bugs? Why or why not?

Get Ready to Listen

Let's learn the **key words**.

A Read and listen to the sentences. Look up the words you don't know in your dictionary. 🔊 103

1. We need **electricity** to make machines work.
2. We all need to help look after the **environment**.
3. The **pollution** in the oceans makes the water dirty.
4. We can **recycle** paper, plastic, and glass.
5. Put your plastic bottles in the **recycling bin**.
6. Maya tries to **reduce** her use of plastic bags.
7. My dad likes to **reuse** old newspapers to clean windows.
8. Mrs. Patel put some **solar panels** on the roof of her house.

B Listen and number. 🔊 104

C Listen and complete the sentences. 🔊 105

There is a lot of (1) _____ in the air near our house because we live near a busy road with lots of cars. My mom says we could (2) _____ it by using our bicycles instead of cars. My old bicycle is broken, but I'm going to (3) _____ it and get another one. I want to do everything I can to help the (4) _____.

Listen

LISTENING GOAL: Listen for Complaints

A complaint is a statement that something is wrong or not good. A complaint can be about a thing, a person, or a situation. Listen for complaints to know how someone feels.

A Listen. What is the speaker's complaint? Choose the correct answer. 🔊 106

1. ☐ a. He bought the TV in the store. ☐ b. His TV isn't working.
2. ☐ a. He can't use the computer. ☐ b. He wants a new computer game.
3. ☐ a. There is trash outside the restaurant. ☐ b. The pizza is too expensive.

The Three Rs ♻♻♻

B Listen to the letter *The Three Rs*. What is it about? Take notes. 🔊 107

Notes

In Alfie's letter, where is his **complaint**?

Now put the sentences in order.

a. Alfie suggests making things from reused plastic. ☐

b. Alfie watches a documentary about pollution in the oceans. ☐

c. Alfie suggests thinking about electricity next year. ☐

Understand

A Think about **The Three Rs**. Answer the questions and discuss with the class.

1. What is Alfie's complaint about?

2. Why does Alfie think his complaint is important?

3. What is Alfie's suggestion to fix the problem?

B Listen to **The Three Rs** again. Choose the correct answer. 108

1. Where does Alfie learn about pollution in the oceans?

   ☐ a. from a TV documentary
   ☐ b. from his mother
   ☐ c. from school lessons
   ☐ d. from an after-school club

2. What is Alfie's first project for the after-school club?

   ☐ a. to learn how to make electricity
   ☐ b. to make videos about recycling
   ☐ c. to build recycling bins
   ☐ d. to buy recycling bins

3. How will they tell other students how to reduce the number of plastic bags and bottles?

   ☐ a. by writing a letter
   ☐ b. by watching a documentary
   ☐ c. by making posters and videos
   ☐ d. by making things from plastic

4. How does Alfie suggest they can reuse plastic?

   ☐ a. by making new things from old plastic bottles
   ☐ b. by using solar panels
   ☐ c. by making videos
   ☐ d. by making electricity

C Read the sentences. Then listen to **The Three Rs** again. Choose the correct answer. 109

1. The principal of the school is **Mr. Long** / **Mr. Smith** / **Mr. Arnold**.

2. Alfie suggests making **2** / **3** / **4** different kinds of recycling bins.

3. Next year, Alfie wants to think about the **weather** / **electricity** / **recycling**.

4. Alfie is in **4th** / **5th** / **6th** grade.

D Ask and answer the questions with a partner.

1. What do you recycle?

2. How could you or your family reduce how much plastic you use?

3. Is it always easy to recycle something? Why or why not?

E Listen and complete the sentences. 🔊 110

| the environment | recycled | reduced | reused |
| pollution | recycling bins | electricity | solar panels |

1. I'm doing a school project about _____

2. Luis decided to buy some _____ for his house.

3. My homework is about _____

4. I've _____ the number of plastic bags I use.

5. Do you have any _____

6. Anjan looked online for ways to help _____

7. Have you ever _____ a plastic bag?

8. Elena _____ her plastic bottle.

F Listen to a woman talking about a recycling project. Fill in the information. 🔊 111

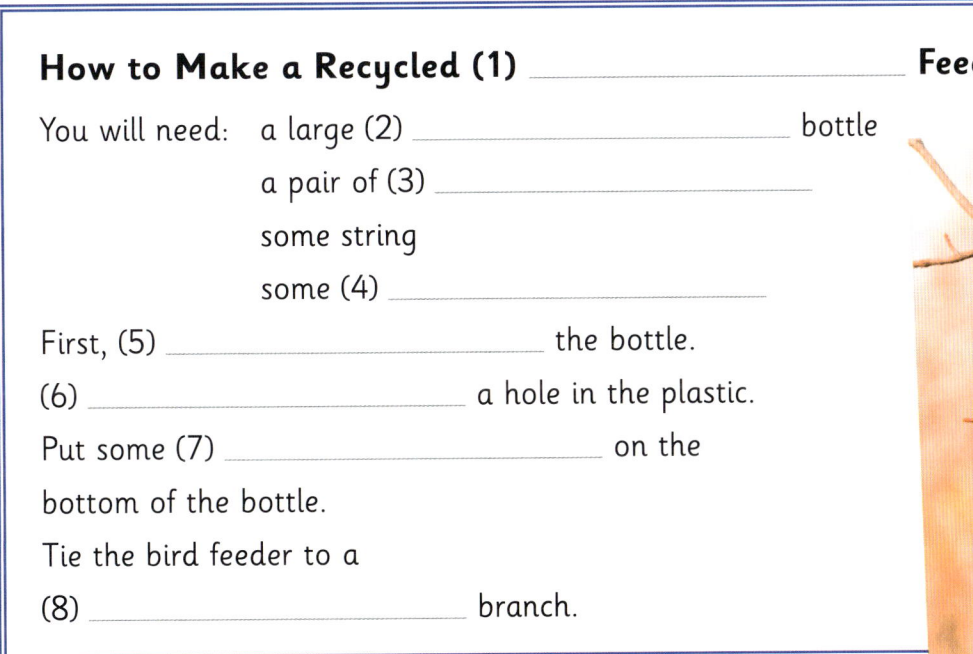

How to Make a Recycled (1) _____ **Feeder**

You will need: a large (2) _____ bottle

a pair of (3) _____

some string

some (4) _____

First, (5) _____ the bottle.

(6) _____ a hole in the plastic.

Put some (7) _____ on the

bottom of the bottle.

Tie the bird feeder to a

(8) _____ branch.

WHAT CAN YOU DO? Color the stars.

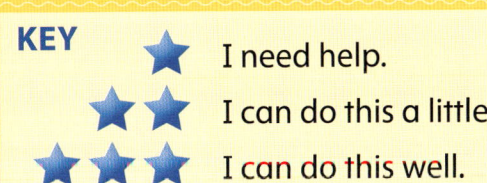
I can listen for complaints to understand how someone feels about something. ⭐⭐⭐

KEY ⭐ I need help.
⭐⭐ I can do this a little.
⭐⭐⭐ I can do this well.

Get Ready to Listen

Let's learn the **key words**.

A Read and listen to the sentences. Look up the words you don't know in your dictionary. 🔊 112

1. Hasan put all the dirty plates in the **dishwasher**.
2. Jo put the wet clothes in the **dryer** and turned it on.
3. We use **energy-saving light bulbs** in our lamps.
4. I put some **fuel** in the car.
5. If you **grow your own vegetables**, you don't have to buy them.
6. Min always **shuts off the water** as he's brushing his teeth.
7. We don't have a car. We **take public transportation**.
8. Please **turn off the lights** when you leave the room.

B Listen and write the number under the picture. 🔊 113

a. _____

b. _____

c. _____

d. _____

C Read each sentence. Then listen. Two of the three key words are incorrect. Write the correct key word. 🔊 114

1. This is a machine that cleans your plates and cups. _____
2. This is what you should do when you brush your teeth. _____
3. This is an activity you can do in your garden. _____
4. This is what makes your car go. _____

Listen

LISTENING GOAL: Listen for Reasons

A reason explains why someone thinks the way they do. People give reasons to help others understand their thinking. Listen for the word *because* to know someone's reason for their thinking.

A Listen and choose the correct answer. 🔊 115

1. Katy was unhappy because no one had **turned on the dishwasher** / **turned off the lights**.

2. Chen doesn't need to buy fuel because he is **taking public transportation** / **walking to work** today.

How Do You Help?

B Listen to the interview *How Do You Help?* What is it about? Take notes. 🔊 116

Notes

Now read. Choose **T** for **True** or **F** for **False**.

1. Rosie is interviewing people in their homes.   T   F

2. The people are telling Rosie how they help the environment.   T   F

3. The people all want to help the environment.   T   F

What is the first man's **reason** for recycling?

WHAT CAN YOU DO?   Color the stars.

I can listen for reasons. ⭐⭐⭐

I can understand all of the key words. ⭐⭐⭐

KEY   I need help.
 I can do this a little.
 I can do this well.

Understand

Remember!
Listen for the word *because*. It is often used when explaining a **reason**.

A Think about **How Do You Help?** Answer the questions and discuss with the class.

1. Why does the second person grow her own vegetables?
2. Why does the third person turn off the lights?
3. Why doesn't the last person use a dryer?
4. Do all of the people give a reason for what they do?

B Listen to **How Do You Help?** again. Choose **T** for **True** or **F** for **False**. 🔊 117

1. Rosie is interviewing people in New Zealand.	T	F
2. Rosie is a teacher.	T	F
3. The first man says he recycles three things in his house.	T	F
4. The woman says some vegetables come from far away.	T	F
5. The man and his daughter try to save electricity and water.	T	F
6. The girl turns off the lights when she brushes her teeth.	T	F
7. The last woman prefers to dry her clothes in the sun.	T	F
8. The last woman gives two reasons for using a bike.	T	F

C Read the sentences. Then listen to **How Do You Help?** again. Complete the sentences. 🔊 118

1. Rosie speaks to _____ different people.
2. The first man says that a plastic bottle takes _____ years to disappear.
3. The girl saves _____
4. The last woman sold her _____ and bought a bike.

D Ask and answer the questions with a partner.

1. Do you do a lot to help the environment? What more could you do?
2. Is it always easy to use less electricity? Why or why not?
3. If you were a scientist or inventor, what would you make to help the environment?

E Listen. Then read and choose the correct answer. 🔊 119

1. When the girl says *turn off the light*, she means
   - ☐ a. make the room go dark.
   - ☐ b. make the room light up.
   - ☐ c. make the sound louder.
   - ☐ d. turn off the television.

2. When the man says *energy-saving light bulbs*, he means
   - ☐ a. cheaper light bulbs.
   - ☐ b. light bulbs that use less electricity.
   - ☐ c. traditional light bulbs.
   - ☐ d. light bulbs that are very small.

3. When the man says *dryer*, he means
   - ☐ a. a machine that dries clothes.
   - ☐ b. a machine that washes clothes.
   - ☐ c. a machine that washes dishes.
   - ☐ d. a machine that dries dishes.

4. When the woman says *public transportation*, she means
   - ☐ a. taxis.
   - ☐ b. a vehicle that you keep at your house.
   - ☐ c. airplanes.
   - ☐ d. vehicles that anyone can travel in.

F Look and listen. Choose the best description. 🔊 120

1.

☐ a. ☐ b. ☐ c. ☐ d.

2.

☐ a. ☐ b. ☐ c. ☐ d.

3.

☐ a. ☐ b. ☐ c. ☐ d.

4.

☐ a. ☐ b. ☐ c. ☐ d.

WHAT CAN YOU DO? Color the stars.

I can listen for reasons in conversations about helping the environment.
⭐⭐⭐

KEY
⭐ I need help.
⭐⭐ I can do this a little.
⭐⭐⭐ I can do this well.

Listening Check

Remember!
People make **complaints** when they think something is wrong or not good. Listen for the **reason** to find out why the person is making complaints and how they feel.

A Listen to the story **A Camping Trip**. What is it about?
Take notes and choose the correct answer. 🔊 121

Notes

_____

_____

_____

_____

☐ a. The children make many complaints.

☐ b. The children learn to enjoy camping.

B Listen to **A Camping Trip** again. Order the pictures. 🔊 122

a.
☐

b.
☐

c.
☐

C Think about **A Camping Trip**. Then choose the correct answer.

1. You want to know how the children are feeling. What should you do?

  ☐ a. listen for complaints   ☐ b. listen for reasons

2. You want to know why the children make complaints. What should you do?

  ☐ a. listen for complaints   ☐ b. listen for reasons

D Answer the questions and discuss your answers with the class.

1. What kinds of things are the children's complaints about?

2. Are they still making complaints at the end of the trip? Why or why not?

E Listen to **A Camping Trip** again. Choose the correct answer. 🔊 123

1. Where is the family camping?
   - ☐ a. at a campsite
   - ☐ b. at their home
   - ☐ c. by the sea
   - ☐ d. by a lake

2. Why are the stars so bright?
   - ☐ a. It is night.
   - ☐ b. There are no city lights.
   - ☐ c. There are lots of them.
   - ☐ d. The family has flashlights.

3. What did the children recycle to make a fridge?
   - ☐ a. a bucket
   - ☐ b. a chair
   - ☐ c. a suitcase
   - ☐ d. a box

4. Who suggests solar panels?
   - ☐ a. Dan
   - ☐ b. Bella
   - ☐ c. Jackie
   - ☐ d. Chris

F Discuss with a partner.

1. Would you like to go camping without electricity? Why or why not?
2. How would you feel about not having a cell phone for five days?
3. Why do you think Dan and Bella start to enjoy the camping trip?

G Listen and read. Complete the sentences. 🔊 124

For my science homework, I have to suggest ways that a family can help the (1) _____. My first suggestion is that they use (2) _____, because then they will save money, too. To save water they should take shorter showers and always remember to (3) _____. And they shouldn't use the (4) _____. To save electricity, they shouldn't use the (5) _____ and they should remember to (6) _____. They could put (7) _____ on the roof of their house. And my final suggestion is that they (8) _____.

WHAT CAN YOU DO? Color the stars.

I can listen for complaints. ⭐⭐⭐
I can listen for reasons. ⭐⭐⭐

KEY
⭐ I need help.
⭐⭐ I can do this a little.
⭐⭐⭐ I can do this well.

Get Ready to Speak

SPEAKING GOAL: Make an Apology

An apology is saying you are sorry that you did something wrong or caused a problem.

A Read and listen to the conversation. Underline the apologies.  125

> **Speaking Tip**
> Use phrases such as *I'm sorry* or *I apologize for* when you make an apology.

Adam: Hey, Mom, I'm back from the store. I bought the candles. Here they are.

Mom: Adam, look at all of these! How many did you buy?

Adam: Ninety.

Mom: No, Adam, I said 19. They're for your sister's birthday cake, and she's only 19 years old tomorrow, not 90!

Adam: Oops, I'm sorry.

Mom: That's okay. Did you get the cake from the bakery?

Adam: Ah, I forgot the cake. I bought a birthday card, though.

Mom: No cake? Your sister loves birthday cake.

Adam: I apologize for getting everything wrong!

Mom: Don't worry. I know! Let's *make* a cake instead.

Adam: Great idea, Mom.

B Discuss the questions with a partner.

1. What does Adam apologize for first?

2. What does Adam apologize for next?

3. What do Adam and his mom decide to do?

NATURAL SPEECH: Numbers

Numbers ending in *–teen* and *–ty* sound similar, but you pronounce the second syllables differently.

15 / 50   13 / 30 126

Listen for **numbers** in **A**. Then practice saying these numbers with a partner.

14 / 40   16 / 60   18 / 80

Speak

C Think about making a mistake or causing a problem. How will you apologize? Write your ideas.

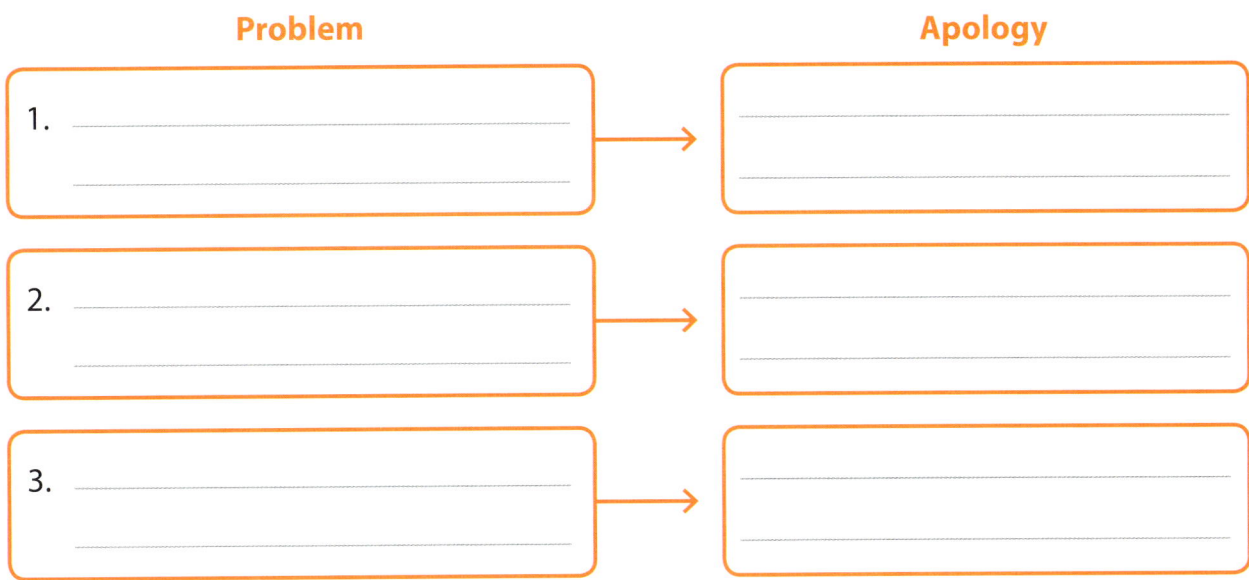

	Problem	Apology
1.		
2.		
3.		

D Write a conversation that includes an apology. Use your words from **C**. Choose new words, too.

1. What is the problem?

2. Which apology phrase are you going to use?

3. How can you resolve the problem?

4. What is the response from the other person?

 Read your conversation to the class or a partner.

WHAT CAN YOU DO? Color the stars.

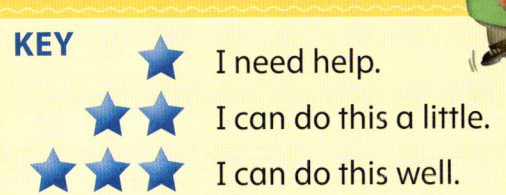

I can apologize. ★★★

I can use apology phrases. ★★★

KEY
★ I need help.
★★ I can do this a little.
★★★ I can do this well.

Let's Learn New Things!

MY GOALS

UNIT 11

- Listen to the conversation *Santiago Today*
- Listen for offers and invitations

UNIT 12

- Listen to the story *A Robot Challenge*
- Listen for refusals

SPEAK

- Make offers and invitations

A Look at the picture.

1. How are these video games different?
2. What do you think the video games are about?

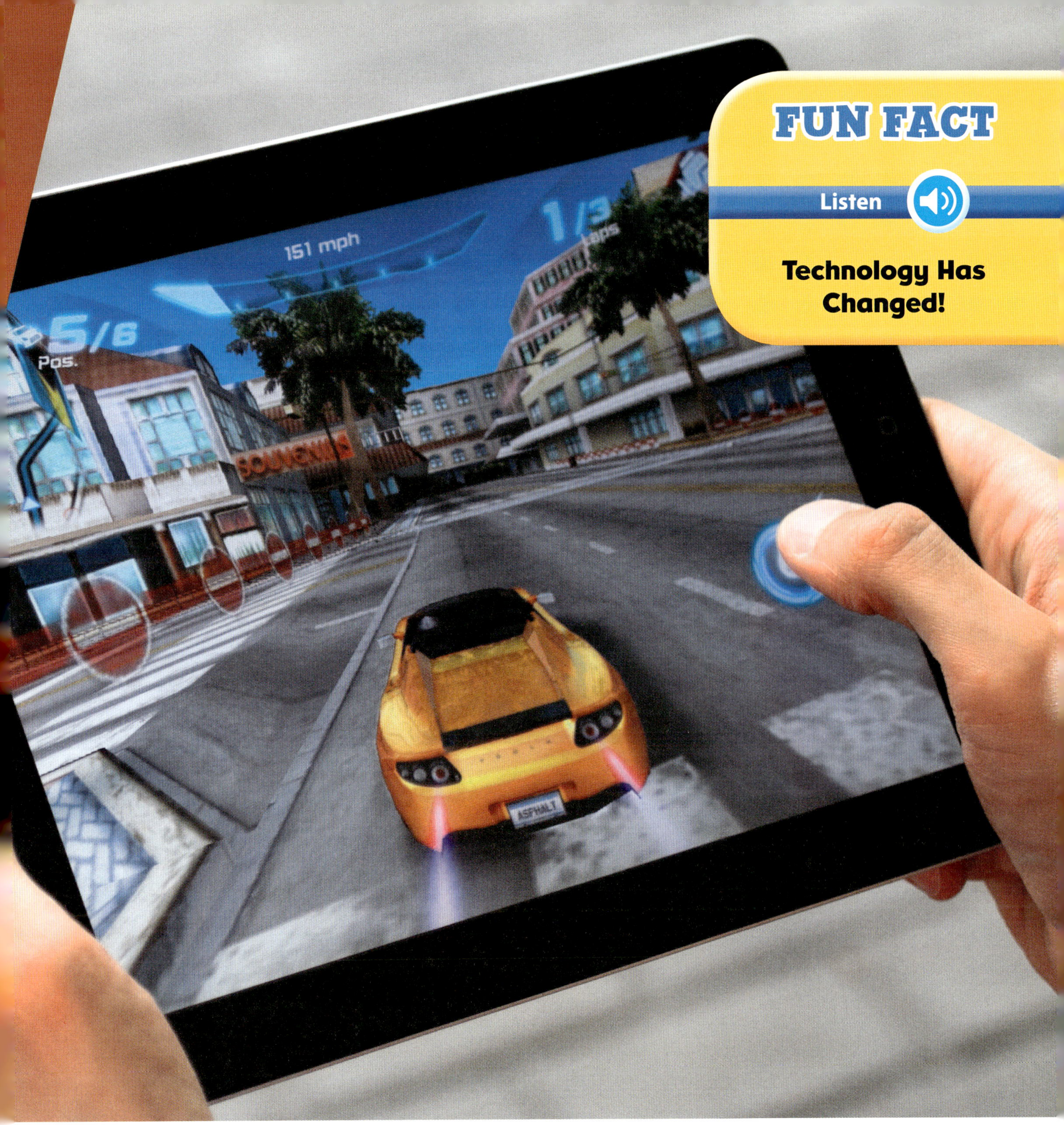

151 mph

1/3 laps

5/6
Pos.

B Listen to the Fun Fact. Then answer the questions. 🔊 127

1. What is the video game on the left called?

2. What year did it come out?

3. How are video games today different?

Think, Pair, Share
Would you like to play these games? Why or why not?

Get Ready to Listen

Let's learn the **key words**.

A Read and listen to the sentences. Look up the words you don't know in your dictionary. 🔊 128

1. Let's **do a workshop** to learn how to play different drums.
2. Holly decided to **go on a bus tour** around Singapore.
3. Do you want to **go to a concert** tonight? It's a rock concert!
4. Li wants to **go to a lecture** about space by a real astronaut.
5. Fiona is **going to an exhibition** about dinosaurs today.
6. You can **visit a film studio** to see where movies are made.
7. We **visited a science museum** and saw a meteorite!
8. I **went to a food festival** last week. I ate a lot of cheese!

B Listen and number. 🔊 129

C Listen and complete the sentences. 🔊 130

Next week, I'm going to (1) _____ by the author of my favorite book. I'm very excited! And afterward, I'm going to (2) _____ on writing short stories. My sister is going to (3) _____ to see its special exhibition about science fiction movies, which she loves. And we're both going to (4) _____. It's our favorite place.

Listen

LISTENING GOAL: Listen for Offers and Invitations

An offer is when someone says they will help, give something, or do something. An invitation is a request to go somewhere. Listen for phrases like *Would you like* to identify offers and invitations.

A Listen. Is the speaker making an offer or an invitation? Choose the correct answer. 🔊 131

1. ☐ a. offer
   ☐ b. invitation

2. ☐ a. offer
   ☐ b. invitation

3. ☐ a. offer
   ☐ b. invitation

Santiago Today

B Listen to the conversation *Santiago Today*. What is it about? Take notes. 🔊 132

Notes

_____

_____

_____

_____

_____

_____

Now put the sentences in order.

What is the **offer** and what is the **invitation**?

a. They are going to go to a food festival at La Vega Market. ☐

b. They are going to do a poetry workshop. ☐

c. They are going to go to an exhibition about spiders. ☐

WHAT CAN YOU DO? Color the stars.

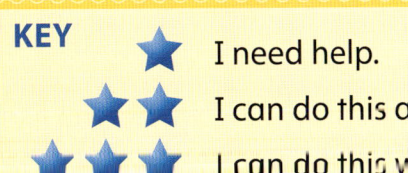

I can listen for offers and invitations. ⭐⭐⭐

I can understand all of the key words. ⭐⭐⭐

KEY
⭐ I need help.
⭐⭐ I can do this a little.
⭐⭐⭐ I can do this well.

Understand

A Think about **Santiago Today**. Answer the questions and discuss with the class.

1. What does Carla invite Sofia to do?

2. What does Carla say when she offers help?

3. What does Sofia say to the invitation and offer?

B Listen to **Santiago Today** again. Choose the correct answer. 🔊 133

1. Where do Carla and Sofia find things to do in Santiago?

- [ ] a. on a TV show
- [ ] b. in a travel book
- [ ] c. in a magazine
- [ ] d. on a website

2. Why can't they go to the lecture or the concert?

- [ ] a. They're not happening on Saturday.
- [ ] b. They finish too late.
- [ ] c. They're too expensive.
- [ ] d. They start too early.

3. What does Carla offer to help Sofia with?

- [ ] a. reading a magazine
- [ ] b. finding an activity to do
- [ ] c. eating burritos
- [ ] d. writing poems

4. Where is the exhibition?

- [ ] a. La Vega Market
- [ ] b. the film studio
- [ ] c. the theater
- [ ] d. the science museum

C Read the sentences. Then listen to **Santiago Today** again. Choose the correct answer. 🔊 134

1. Sofia's family is catching the **6 a.m.** / **9 a.m.** / **6 p.m.** train to Santiago.

2. The food festival is about **French** / **Chinese** / **Mexican** food.

3. There's a lecture about **space travel** / **classical music** / **spiders**.

4. Sofia and Carla went on a bus tour around Santiago **last month** / **last year** / **last week**.

D Ask and answer the questions with a partner.

1. What activities have you done recently? Which did you enjoy most?

2. What new thing would you like to learn about?

3. What concert would you like to go to? Why?

E Listen and complete the sentences. 🔊 135

visited the science museum	did a workshop	went on a bus tour
visiting the film studio	go to an exhibition	went to a lecture
go to the concert	go to a food festival

1. Would you like to _____ with me next week?

2. I couldn't _____ because I was sick.

3. Mr. and Mrs. Brown _____ and took lots of photos.

4. Julian _____ at the town hall last night.

5. We _____ about how to make a short cartoon. It was very interesting.

6. I love _____ in Los Angeles. I've been there five times!

7. I've never _____, but I'd love to go.

8. Every year we _____ in our town.

F Listen to an advertisement for a food festival. Fill in the information. 🔊 136

Food Festival!

When: Saturday – (1) _____

Opens at: (2) _____

Foods: (3) _____ from Japan, curry from (4) _____, (5) _____ from Italy

Cooking demo: learn to make spicy chicken (6) _____ and how to use (7) _____

WHAT CAN YOU DO? Color the stars.

I can identify offers and invitations in a conversation. ⭐⭐⭐

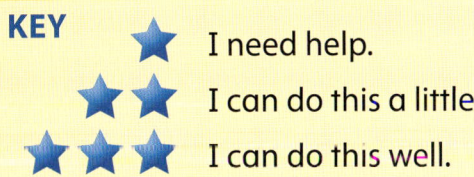

KEY ⭐ I need help.
⭐⭐ I can do this a little.
⭐⭐⭐ I can do this well.

Get Ready to Listen

Let's learn the **key words**.

A Read and listen to the sentences. Look up the words you don't know in your dictionary. 🔊 137

1. I learned how to make a cup with my **3D printer**.
2. Chris flew his **drone** around the garden.
3. Let's **go to a website** that will help us with our homework.
4. Sarah always goes **offline** two hours before her bedtime.
5. I use my **smartwatch** to check my e-mails.
6. My computer has **software** for drawing pictures.
7. Ann played a video game on her **virtual reality headset**.
8. I want to learn how to **write code** to make a video game.

B Listen and write the number under the picture. 🔊 138

a. _____

b. _____

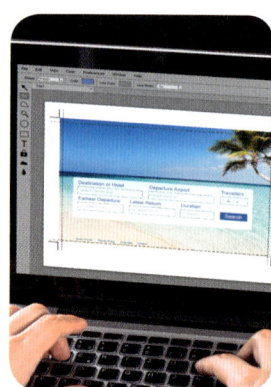

c. _____

d. _____

C Read each sentence. Then listen. Two of the three key words are incorrect. Write the correct key word. 🔊 139

1. You can wear this machine on your head to see an electronic world. _____
2. This is a machine that you can fly without a pilot. _____
3. This is a machine that can make things from plastic. _____
4. This is a computer that you wear on your arm. _____

Listen

LISTENING GOAL: Listen for Refusals

A refusal is saying no to an offer or an invitation. Listen for words and phrases like *Thank you, but* and *I'm sorry, but* to identify refusals.

A Listen and choose the correct answer. 🔊 140

1. Jane wants **some pizza** / **an apple**.
2. The boys are going to watch a movie **this afternoon** / **tomorrow**.

A Robot Challenge

B Listen to the story *A Robot Challenge*.
What happens? Take notes. 🔊 141

Notes

_____

_____

_____

_____

_____

_____

> What phrases does Suki use to **refuse** the children's offers?

Now read. Choose T for True or F for False.

1.	Rachel is a robot.	T	F
2.	Rachel and Tommy want Suki to play with them.	T	F
3.	Rachel and Tommy learn how to write code.	T	F

WHAT CAN YOU DO? Color the stars.

I can listen for refusals. ★★★

I can understand all of the key words. ★★★

KEY
★ I need help.
★★ I can do this a little.
★★★ I can do this well.

Understand

Remember!
A **refusal** is saying no to an offer or an invitation.

A Think about **A Robot Challenge**.
Answer the questions and discuss with the class.

1. What is Tommy's first offer?

2. What reason does Suki give for refusing the second offer?

3. Why is Suki really refusing all their offers to play?

4. What offer does Suki accept in the end?

B Listen to **A Robot Challenge** again. Choose **T** for **True** or **F** for **False**. 🔊 142

		T	F
1.	Suki does lots of chores in the house.	T	F
2.	Rachel has a virtual reality headset.	T	F
3.	Rachel and Tommy build a drone on their 3D printer.	T	F
4.	Rachel uses a smartwatch to go to a website.	T	F
5.	The children learn how to write code offline.	T	F
6.	Tommy changes the piece of code in Suki's software.	T	F
7.	Suki accepts Tommy's offer to play soccer.	T	F
8.	The children go to the beach with Suki.	T	F

C Read the sentences. Then listen to **A Robot Challenge** again.
Complete the sentences. 🔊 143

1. Suki refuses to play chess because she has _____ to do.

2. The children spend _____ days learning how to write code.

3. Rachel finds the piece of code in the robot's _____

4. The children and Suki fly kites, _____, and make sandcastles.

D Ask and answer the questions with a partner.

1. Do you want to learn how to write code?
   What would you write code for?

2. Would you like to have a robot in your house?
   Why or why not?

3. What do you think technology will be like in
   30 years? What gadgets will we have?

Listen. Then read and choose the correct answer. 🔊 144

1. When the girl says *offline*, she means
   - ☐ a. connected to the Internet.
   - ☐ b. using a computer.
   - ☐ c. using a tablet.
   - ☐ d. not connected to the Internet.

2. When the man says *drone*, he means
   - ☐ a. a plane without a pilot.
   - ☐ b. an airplane.
   - ☐ c. a camera on a cell phone.
   - ☐ d. a boat.

3. When the boy says *software*, he means
   - ☐ a. a robot.
   - ☐ b. the Internet.
   - ☐ c. a computer program.
   - ☐ d. a computer.

4. When the woman says *smartwatch*, she means
   - ☐ a. a watch that looks beautiful.
   - ☐ b. a smartphone with a watch.
   - ☐ c. a watch with a small computer inside.
   - ☐ d. a laptop with a clock on the screen.

F **Look and listen. Choose the best description.** 🔊 145

1.
☐ a. ☐ b. ☐ c. ☐ d.

2.
☐ a. ☐ b. ☐ c. ☐ d.

3.
☐ a. ☐ b. ☐ c. ☐ d.

4.
☐ a. ☐ b. ☐ c. ☐ d.

WHAT CAN YOU DO? Color the stars.

I can listen for refusals of offers and invitations in a story. ★★★

KEY
★ I need help.
★★ I can do this a little.
★★★ I can do this well.

Listening Check

Remember!
You can make an **offer** or **invitation** with *Would you like*? To **refuse** an offer or invitation, you can use *Thank you, but* and *I'm sorry, but*.

A Listen to the conversation **A Day Out**. What is it about? Take notes and choose the correct answer. 🔊 146

Notes

_____

_____

_____

_____

☐ a. Magda is inviting Clarissa to go to a film studio with her.

☐ b. Clarissa wants to tell Magda what they can do at the film studio.

B Listen to **A Day Out** again. Order the pictures. 🔊 147

a. ☐   b. ☐   c. ☐

C Think about **A Day Out**. Then choose the correct answer.

1. You want to know what Magda would like Clarissa to do. What should you do?

   ☐ a. listen for offers and invitations   ☐ b. listen for refusals

2. You want to know what Clarissa doesn't want to do. What should you do?

   ☐ a. listen for offers and invitations   ☐ b. listen for refusals

D Answer the questions and discuss your answers with the class.

1. What did Clarissa do the first time Madga invited her to the studios?

2. What did Clarissa do the second time Magda invited her?

E Listen to **A Day Out** again. Choose the correct answer. 🔊 148

1. Where do they read about the film studio?

   ☐ a. a magazine

   ☐ b. a website

   ☐ c. an invitation

   ☐ d. an e-mail

2. What sport can they do in virtual reality?

   ☐ a. golf

   ☐ b. tai chi

   ☐ c. table tennis

   ☐ d. judo

3. What is the workshop about?

   ☐ a. music

   ☐ b. special effects

   ☐ c. the actor

   ☐ d. the film studio

4. What does Clarissa offer to do?

   ☐ a. bring lunch

   ☐ b. look online

   ☐ c. go to a lecture

   ☐ d. play music

F Discuss with a partner.

1. Which actor would you like to meet? Why?

2. How do you find information about things to do in your town?

3. When should you refuse an invitation?

G Listen and read. Complete the sentences. 🔊 149

There are a lot of ways to learn new things. Some of them are online. You can (1) _____ and learn a new skill, such as how to (2) _____ or use new (3) _____

And some ways to learn are offline. For example, you can (4) _____ Sometimes they have a (5) _____ so you can see what it is like in space or on the International Space Station! Or you can (6) _____ or (7) _____. Another great way to learn things is to (8) _____. Then you can actually try it for yourself.

WHAT CAN YOU DO? Color the stars.

I can listen for invitations and offers.

⭐⭐⭐

I can listen for refusals.

⭐⭐⭐

KEY   ⭐ I need help.

⭐⭐ I can do this a little.

⭐⭐⭐ I can do this well.

Get Ready to Speak

SPEAKING GOAL: Make Offers and Invitations

An offer is when someone says they will help, give something, or do something. An invitation is a request to go somewhere or do something.

A Read and listen to the conversation. Underline the offers and circle the invitations.  150

> **Speaking Tip**
> Use *Would you like* to make offers and invitations.

Dad: Molly, would you like to play golf with me tomorrow? I can teach you how to play.

Molly: I already know how to play golf, Dad.

Dad: Really? How did you learn?

Molly: I have a golfing video game. It's great, and I'm really good at it. Would you like to play with me?

Dad: Oh, well, I'm not very good at video games.

Molly: Would you like me to show you how? I can teach you.

Dad: You can? I never thought my daughter would teach me golf! You turn the video game on, and I'll get us some drinks. Would you like juice?

Molly: Yes, please!

Dad: Okay, let's get started!

B Discuss the questions with a partner.

1. What does Dad invite Molly to do?
2. What does Molly offer to do?
3. Does Dad refuse any of Molly's offers?

 NATURAL SPEECH: *Can*

When we say *can* within a sentence, it is unstressed. But when we say *can* at the end of a sentence, it is stressed.

I can teach you how to play golf.   You **can**? 151

Listen for *can* in **A**. Then write a sentence with *can* in the middle and a sentence with *can* at the end. Say them with stress to your partner.

Speak

C Think about something you would like to teach someone. Think about how you could offer to help them.

Offer to help

Thing to teach

Offer to help

Offer to help

D Write a conversation and offer to help someone learn something new. Use your words from **C**. Choose new words, too.

1. What is the thing you want to teach?

2. What will the person need to learn to do the thing?

3. How can you offer to help?

4. How could the person respond to your offer?

 Work with a partner. Offer to teach him or her something new.

WHAT CAN YOU DO? Color the stars.

I can make offers and invitations.
★★★

I can use *Would you like.*
★★★

KEY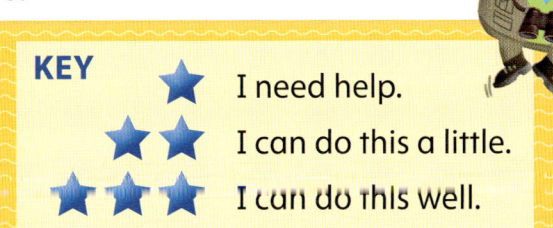
★ I need help.
★★ I can do this a little.
★★★ I can do this well.

Listening

WITH Speaking

6

Workbook

Joanna Ross

OXFORD
UNIVERSITY PRESS

Listen

LISTENING GOAL:
Listen for Key Information

Remember!
Words or phrases that you hear many times are important. They are key information. Listen for **key information** to know what a listening is about.

A Listen to the phone call **A Delicious Lunch**. What is it about? Take notes. Then choose **T** for **True** or **F** for **False**. 🔊 152

Notes

_____

_____

_____

_____

_____

1. The phone call is about two women planning to meet for lunch.   (T)   F
2. They both enjoyed a meal in the Turkish restaurant last year.   T   F
3. The women can't agree on a new place to meet.   T   F

B Think about **A Delicious Lunch**. Which is key information? Choose the correct answer.

☐ a. Amanda doesn't like Parmesan cheese.

☐ b. The women decide to go to the Turkish restaurant.

☐ c. Jefferson Avenue is a one-way street.

C Listen to **A Delicious Lunch** again. Choose the correct answer. 🔊 153

1. When are the women going to meet?

   ☐ a. today

   ☑ b. tomorrow

   ☐ c. next week

2. Which restaurant does Amanda say sounds really good?

   ☐ a. the Turkish restaurant

   ☐ b. the French restaurant

   ☐ c. the Italian restaurant

3. Which restaurant has a famous chef?

   ☐ a. the Turkish restaurant

   ☐ b. the French restaurant

   ☐ c. the Italian restaurant

4. The Turkish restaurant is across from which building?

   ☐ a. the bookstore

   ☐ b. the French restaurant

   ☐ c. the bank

D Think about **A Delicious Lunch** again. Answer the questions. Use full sentences.

1. Why does Josie need to be downtown?

   Josie needs to be downtown because she has a dentist appointment.

2. Why doesn't Amanda like Italian food?

   _____

3. How do you get to the Turkish restaurant from the bookstore?

   _____

4. Why do the women like the Turkish restaurant?

   _____

5. What did Amanda eat at the Turkish restaurant last year?

   _____

6. What did the women forget to agree on?

   _____

E Listen. Choose the correct answer. 🔊 154

1. My favorite stores are **downtown** / **uptown**.
2. Park Road is a **one-way street** / **dead end**.
3. I cross the road at the **intersection** / **one-way street**.
4. **Hurry to** / **Go past** the bus stop.
5. Camilla's dance school is **uptown** / **around the corner**.
6. My uncle's restaurant is on Main Street at **an intersection** / **a dead end**.

F Listen and read. Complete the sentences. 🔊 155

"Oh, no, I'm lost!" thought Alia. She was trying to reach the toy store to buy a present for her friend's birthday, but it was already 4:30 and the store closed at 5 p.m. She needed to (1) _____hurry_____. She knew the toy store was (2) _____ the (3) _____, but she didn't know which way to turn. She turned right, but it was a (4) _____. She decided to turn left, instead, and suddenly she knew where she was. "Ah, this is Elm Street. I just need to (5) _____ post office and I'll be there." Alia walked quickly down the street. "Next time I'm (6) _____, I'll bring a map!"

Listen

LISTENING GOAL:
Listen and Take Notes —
Cornell Method

> **Remember!**
> The **Cornell Method** is a form of note-taking. Write key information on the left and notes for the key information on the right. Then write a one-line summary.

A Listen to the story **A Secret Vacation**. Complete the table using the Cornell Method. 🔊 156

Key Information	Notes
1. swimsuit	clothing store, past candy store, turn right
2.	
3.	

B Think about **A Secret Vacation**. Which is the best summary?

☐ a. The girls play a game where they buy three items for their vacation.

☐ b. Mom and Dad find out how much each item costs in each store.

☐ c. The girls don't like shopping but they like camping.

C Listen to **A Secret Vacation** again. Choose the correct answer. 🔊 157

1. Samantha and Serena love school.
   ☐ a. true   ☐ b. false   ☑ c. doesn't say

2. The girls love shopping.
   ☐ a. true   ☐ b. false   ☐ c. doesn't say

3. Two swimsuits will cost $40.
   ☐ a. true   ☐ b. false   ☐ c. doesn't say

4. They can buy hot dogs at the grocery store.
   ☐ a. true   ☐ b. false   ☐ c. doesn't say

5. The tent costs more than $40.
   ☐ a. true   ☐ b. false   ☐ c. doesn't say

D Think about **A Secret Vacation**. Complete the sentences with one, two, or three words.

1. Samantha and Serena think _____shopping_____ is boring.

2. Dad says they are going to play _____

3. The girls have to buy _____ things.

4. The first item is _____ for each girl.

5. A pack of _____ costs about $3.

6. For their vacation, the family is going _____

E Listen and read. Choose the correct answer. 🔊 158

> The most interesting store in my town is the (1) _____ because it sells everything you could need to build a tree house. To get there, you walk (2) _____ the park and turn right. Then go past the (3) _____. On the way back home, you can stop at the (4) _____ if you have any money left!

1. ☑ a. hardware store   2. ☐ a. beyond
   ☐ b. grocery store   ☐ b. toward

3. ☐ a. grocery store   4. ☐ a. candy store
   ☐ b. candy store   ☐ b. park

F Listen and complete the sentences. 🔊 159

1. The _____grocery store_____ is open from 9 a.m. to 5 p.m. every day.

2. The hardware store is _____

3. The park is _____ from my house.

4. Can you see the school? It's just _____ the parking lot.

5. Walk _____ the intersection.

6. To get to the bank, _____ and turn right.

Speak

**Circle the most interesting introduction sentence.
Tell your partner why you like it.**

My favorite walk is to the park.

I love the dentist. Yes, really! I walk to the dentist with a smile on my face.

I walk to school every day.

> **Remember!**
> Use a strong introduction sentence when you give a speech.

Listen

LISTENING GOAL:
Listen and Analyze Characters

Remember!
To **analyze characters**, listen carefully to hear what they say and do and how they look.

A Listen to the story **The Exam**. What is it about? Take notes. Then choose **T** for **True** or **F** for **False**. 🔊 160

Notes

_____

_____

_____

_____

1. Jake usually enjoys school. **T   F**
2. Jake studies hard for the exam. **T   F**
3. Jake isn't smart enough to do well in school. **T   F**

B Think about **The Exam**. How do you know that Jake is unhappy before the exam? Choose the correct answers.

☐ a. He changes his normal activities.

☐ b. He's quiet, and he only wants to talk about his game.

☐ c. He says he's unhappy.

C Listen to **The Exam** again. Choose the correct answer. 🔊 161

1. The teacher tells Jake and Ben they should study hard

☐ a. for a few months.

☐ b. for a few days.

☐ c. all the time.

2. What does Jake start doing?

☐ a. making a study plan

☐ b. studying until late at night

☐ c. neither of the above

3. How does Ben feel about the exam?

☐ a. It wasn't easy but he tried hard.

☐ b. He thought he wouldn't do well.

☐ c. He was nervous.

4. Why does Ben think he did well on the exam?

☐ a. because he is really smart

☐ b. because he studied hard

☐ c. because he wasn't sleepy

D Think about **The Exam** again. Answer the questions. Use full sentences.

1. What is Jake usually like at school?

   _____

2. What did Jake do instead of studying?

   _____

3. How did Ben get ready for the exam?

   _____

4. Why do you think Jake ran home without saying goodbye?

   _____

5. Why didn't Jake want to study for the exam?

   _____

6. How did Jake feel after he talked to Ben at the end of the story?

   _____

E Listen. Choose the correct answer. 🔊 162

1. In Japan it is **impolite** / **polite** to take your shoes off before going into a house.
2. Sanjay is **a cheerful** / **an unhappy** man.
3. William is **fascinated by** / **curious about** dinosaurs.
4. I was **sleepy** / **foolish** because I stayed up until 11 p.m. last night.
5. My brother is **unhappy** / **curious** about the big exam next week.
6. Karen was so **sleepy** / **unhappy** in English class this morning.

F Listen and read. Complete the sentences. 🔊 163

Last week my cat had three baby kittens and I was
(1) _____ by them. They all have the same brown
and white stripes, but they are also very different. The biggest
one is called LuLu and she is very (2) _____
about everything. Denzil is the middle one, and he's always
(3) _____. The smallest one is my favorite because
he's very (4) _____ and wants to play all the time.
He isn't shy! He doesn't have a name yet, but I might call him
Lionel because he's as brave as a lion!

Listen

LISTENING GOAL:
Listen and Make Value Judgments

> **Remember!**
> **Value judgments** are opinions about what is right or wrong. When you listen, ask *Did the character do the right thing? What kind of person is the character?*

A Listen to the conversation **Anna's Birthday**. What is it about? Take notes. Then choose the correct answer. 🔊 164

Notes

_____

_____

_____

1. What is *Anna's Birthday* about?

   ☐ a. a boy falling off a roof   ☐ b. how Anna feels about her mom

2. Did Anna enjoy her birthday?

   ☐ a. Yes, she did.   ☐ b. No, she didn't.

B Think about **Anna's Birthday**. What is Anna's value judgment about her mom? Choose the correct answer.

☐ a. She thinks her mom should have come home for her birthday dinner.

☐ b. She thinks her mom did the right thing.

☐ c. She thinks her mom works too hard.

C Listen to **Anna's Birthday** again. Choose the correct answer. 🔊 165

1. Anna is 12 years old.

   ☐ a. true   ☐ b. false   ☐ c. doesn't say

2. Anna's dad cooked eggs for breakfast yesterday.

   ☐ a. true   ☐ b. false   ☐ c. doesn't say

3. Anna's mom is a nurse at the hospital.

   ☐ a. true   ☐ b. false   ☐ c. doesn't say

4. The little boy went to the hospital in an ambulance.

   ☐ a. true   ☐ b. false   ☐ c. doesn't say

5. Anna's mom is sleeping now.

   ☐ a. true   ☐ b. false   ☐ c. doesn't say

D Think about **Anna's Birthday** again. Complete the sentences with one, two, or three words.

1. Anna woke up _____ on her birthday.

2. Her parents gave her a _____

3. A _____ climbed a tree behind his house.

4. He fell and _____

5. Anna's mom got home at _____ this morning.

6. Anna's dad made a _____ for dinner.

E Listen and read. Choose the correct answer. 🔊 166

My hero is James Emery. He has an animal show on TV. He's very (1) _____. I like him because he is very (2) _____. He travels around the world finding out about animals, and sometimes it can be a (3) _____ job. On TV he tells us that he is (4) _____ because we are destroying our planet.

1. ☐ a. cheerful
   ☐ b. popular

2. ☐ a. hilarious
   ☐ b. courageous

3. ☐ a. dangerous
   ☐ b. foolish

4. ☐ a. curious
   ☐ b. worried

F Listen and complete the sentences. 🔊 167

1. Suki looks a little _____. Is she okay?

2. This book is _____. You should read it.

3. I think the girl in the movie is _____ to her brother.

4. My dad said I shouldn't be _____

5. Are you _____ about the storm?

6. Let's watch the new movie. It's very _____

Speak

Underline the metaphor and circle the simile. Think of one more metaphor and one more simile. Tell your partner.

I forgot to wear my gloves, so my fingers feel as cold as ice.

The classroom was a zoo.

> **Remember!**
> A simile uses *like* or *as* to compare two things. A metaphor is a way to compare two things that are not the same but have something in common.

Listen

LISTENING GOAL:
Listen and Make Inferences

Remember!
An **inference** is a guess about what a listening does not tell you. Use clues and what you already know to make an inference.

A Listen to the story **The Language Lesson**. What happens? Take notes. Then choose **T** for **True** or **F** for **False**. 🔊 168

Notes

_____

_____

_____

_____

_____

1. Ella is learning Spanish in an after-school class.   **T**   **F**

2. Ella speaks lots of languages.   **T**   **F**

3. The students in the class like when Ella says a sentence.   **T**   **F**

B Think about **The Language Lesson**. How does Ella feel about her mom? Choose the correct answers.

☐ a. She wants to be smart like her mom.

☐ b. She misses her mom when she is away.

☐ c. She wants her mom to be proud of her.

C Listen to **The Language Lesson** again. Choose the correct answer. 🔊 169

1. Ella's mom can speak

☐ a. five languages.

☐ b. four languages.

☐ c. one language.

2. Her mom will be home

☐ a. next week.

☐ b. in three weeks.

☐ c. in three months.

3. Ella wants to speak Spanish because

☐ a. she wants an amazing job.

☐ b. she wants to travel the world.

☐ c. her mom speaks Spanish.

4. Ella learns

☐ a. how to say her name in Spanish.

☐ b. how to say one new sentence.

☐ c. how to ask a question in Spanish.

D Think about **The Language Lesson** again. Answer the questions. Use full sentences.

1. How does Ella feel when she can't answer the teacher?

   _____

2. How does Ella feel by the end of the lesson?

   _____

3. What is Ella's mother tongue?

   _____

4. Where is Ella's mom?

   _____

5. How does Ella learn to say a whole sentence in Spanish?

   _____

6. What does the class do when Ella says her sentence?

   _____

E Listen. Choose the correct answer. 🔊 170

1. I watched a travel program about **Thailand** / **Vietnam** on TV last night.
2. Have you ever been to **Southeast Asia** / **Vietnam**?
3. My best friend is **Thai** / **Vietnamese**.
4. My sister is **fluent** / **multilingual**.
5. Jeff can speak quickly in **his mother tongue** / **Vietnamese**.
6. Our teacher is **fluent** / **multilingual** in four languages.

F Listen and read. Complete the sentences. 🔊 171

My French teacher, Mr. Martin, is (1) _____. He can
speak three languages! His (2) _____ is French,
but he can also speak English. Surprisingly, he can also speak
(3) _____, but he is not (4) _____.
When he was younger, Mr. Martin spent three years teaching
English and French in (5) _____. While he was
living there, my teacher read the newspaper every day and
spoke to people in stores and cafés. He got better and better
at reading and speaking! I think that is a great way to learn
a language.

Listen

LISTENING GOAL:
Listen and Paraphrase

A Listen to the lecture **American English**. What is it about? Take notes. Then choose the correct answer. 🔊 172

Notes

_____

_____

_____

1. What is *American English* about?

☐ a. what to eat in in London

☐ b. American English and British English

2. Did the teacher enjoy his trip?

☐ a. Yes, he did.

☐ b. No, he didn't.

B Think about **American English**. Why does George paraphrase his teacher? Choose the correct answer.

☐ a. to ask the teacher to repeat the information

☐ b. to check that he understood his teacher correctly

☐ c. to find out some new information

C Listen to **American English** again. Choose the correct answer. 🔊 173

1. The teacher went to London alone.

☐ a. true   ☐ b. false   ☐ c. doesn't say

2. French fries are called *chips* in British English.

☐ a. true   ☐ b. false   ☐ c. doesn't say

3. Rocket is a salad vegetable in British English.

☐ a. true   ☐ b. false   ☐ c. doesn't say

4. The teacher went to an American football game in London.

☐ a. true   ☐ b. false   ☐ c. doesn't say

5. The family had a chicken pie.

☐ a. true   ☐ b. false   ☐ c. doesn't say

D Think about **American English** again. Complete the sentences with one, two, or three words.

1. The teacher is teaching a _____ lesson.

2. People speak _____ in England.

3. A candy store is called a _____ in England.

4. A soccer game is called a _____ match in England.

5. A tomato is called a _____ in England.

6. The teacher had _____ for a snack at the soccer stadium.

E Listen and read. Choose the correct answer. 🔊 174

There is a wonderful (1) _____ restaurant near my house. It has delicious dishes, such as chicken–lemon soup and beef stew. The waiters are all from (2) _____. They don't speak fluent English, but they have big smiles and are good at using (3) _____ for words. I have a (4) _____ on my phone, so I use that if I can't understand a word. It is always a great evening.

1. ☐ a. German   2. ☐ a. Europe   3. ☐ a. gestures   4. ☐ a. dictionary app
   ☐ b. Greek   ☐ b. Greece   ☐ b. a dictionary   ☐ b. translation game

F Listen and complete the sentences. 🔊 175

1. I've never been to _____, but I'd like to visit Rome and Paris.

2. The _____ city of Hamburg is in the north of the country.

3. My homework is to _____ this French text into English.

4. The _____ flag has blue and white stripes.

5. More than 82 million people live in _____

6. Can I use your _____

Speak

> **Remember!**
> When you summarize, include main ideas but not the details of a passage.

Circle the main ideas in the passage. Use the main ideas to write a summary. Tell your partner.

James Dixon enjoyed learning languages at school. When he was 8 he started to learn French. By the age of 11 he was fluent in French and German. In high school he learned Japanese. And in college he studied Arabic and Mandarin. Now he can speak six languages and has a job as a translator on a TV news show.

Listen

LISTENING GOAL:
Listen for the Speaker's Purpose

Remember!
A speaker has a **purpose**, or reason, for speaking. When you listen, ask *Who is speaking?* and *Why is the speaker saying this?*

A Listen to the passage **My Summer Vacation**. What is it about? Take notes. Then choose **T** for **True** or **F** for **False**. 🔊 176

Notes

_____
_____
_____
_____

1. David tells a story about going rock climbing.   **T**   **F**
2. David tells a story about bears at the zoo.   **T**   **F**
3. David tells a story about going caving.   **T**   **F**

B Think about **My Summer Vacation**. What is David's purpose for speaking? Choose the correct answers.

☐ a. He wants the class to enjoy his funny story.

☐ b. He wants to tell the class about a cave in Portugal.

☐ c. He wants to persuade the class to visit the cave.

C Listen to **My Summer Vacation** again. Choose the correct answer. 🔊 177

1. How did David's family travel to Portugal?

 ☐ a. by airplane

 ☐ b. by bus

 ☐ c. by ship

2. What interesting things did David see in the caves?

 ☐ a. spiders and ants

 ☐ b. a rock pool

 ☐ c. stalactites and bats

3. What was it like inside the caves?

 ☐ a. cold and dry

 ☐ b. dark and wet

 ☐ c. sunny

4. What did they do on the next day?

 ☐ a. They went back to the caves.

 ☐ b. They went rafting.

 ☐ c. They went to the beach.

D Think about **My Summer Vacation** again. Answer the questions. Use full sentences.

1. Who did David go on vacation with?

   _____

2. Where was David's hotel?

   _____

3. What safety equipment did they take into the caves?

   _____

4. What safety equipment didn't they take? Why?

   _____

5. What did David do when he saw a bear?

   _____

6. What did David's dad want to do the next day?

   _____

E Listen. Choose the correct answer. 🔊 178

1. You are 3 kilometers high in the sky when you go **skydiving** / **bungee jumping**.
2. You wear a **rope** / **harness** when you go rock climbing.
3. When you go rafting, you can hold on to a **rope** / **harness** on the raft.
4. I was scared when we **rode the roller coaster** / **went bungee jumping**.
5. Since Marla can't swim, she won't **go scuba diving** / **go rafting** with us.
6. We don't have the right equipment to **go caving** / **go scuba diving**.

F Listen and read. Complete the sentences. 🔊 179

My grandfather is going to turn 82 years old this year. For his birthday, he decided that he wants to do some adventure sports. I always spend time with him on his birthday, so I said we should do them together. And I read that the best place in the world for adventure sports is New Zealand! First we are going to (1) _____, which I think will be fun. Then we'll (2) _____ from a bridge. I think that will feel just like a (3) _____. And finally we're going to (4) _____ and (5) _____. After all of that, I think we'll need a vacation!

Listen

LISTENING GOAL:
Listen for Advice

A Listen to the radio show **Travel with Tania**. What is it about? Take notes. Then choose the correct answer. 🔊 180

Notes

_____

_____

_____

_____

1. What is *Travel with Tania* about?

   ☐ a. what to do, see, and eat in Bali

   ☐ b. where to find the best beaches

2. Where is Bali?

   ☐ a. It's an island in Indonesia.

   ☐ b. It's in Australia.

B Think about **Travel with Tania**. Which sentences are advice from Tania? Choose the correct answers.

   ☐ a. It takes two hours to climb Mount Batur.

   ☐ b. You should drink lots of water.

   ☐ c. You should try *nasi goreng*.

C Listen to **Travel with Tania** again. Choose the correct answer. 🔊 181

1. Tania flew from Australia to Bali.

   ☐ a. true   ☐ b. false   ☐ c. doesn't say

2. Tania took two suitcases to Bali.

   ☐ a. true   ☐ b. false   ☐ c. doesn't say

3. The sun is hottest between 11 a.m. and 1 p.m.

   ☐ a. true   ☐ b. false   ☐ c. doesn't say

4. It can get cold climbing the mountain.

   ☐ a. true   ☐ b. false   ☐ c. doesn't say

5. Tania stayed in Bali for two weeks.

   ☐ a. true   ☐ b. false   ☐ c. doesn't say

D Think about **Travel with Tania** again. Complete the sentences with one, two, or three words.

1. Tania's flight was _____

2. The first thing Tania did was go _____

3. The sea is _____

4. You should drink lots of _____

5. Tania climbed a _____ called Mount Batur.

6. *Nasi goreng* means fried _____

E Listen and read. Choose the correct answer. 🔊 182

My name is Audrey and I'm a pilot. After I arrive at the airport, I go through (1) _____ with my (2) _____. I always have my (3) _____ with me. Then I get on the plane and do all the safety checks. I am happy if everything goes well and my flight is (4) _____.

1. ☐ a. security
   ☐ b. the waiting area

2. ☐ a. boarding pass
   ☐ b. carry-on luggage

3. ☐ a. boarding pass
   ☐ b. passport

4. ☐ a. on time
   ☐ b. empty

F Listen and complete the sentences. 🔊 183

1. Do you have your _____

2. Zan's flight to Japan was _____

3. I _____ my money before I traveled.

4. My mom works in _____ at the airport.

5. She went to the _____ area.

6. My _____ is red.

Speak

Underline the advice. Then think of your own advice. Tell your advice to your partner.

There are many things to do and see in Japan. Do you want to visit Japan? Then you should plan a trip! Make sure you have a passport. You should exchange your money for yen, too.

Remember!
Use *should* when giving advice.

Listen

LISTENING GOAL:
Listen for Complaints

A Listen to the story **A Beautiful Garden**. What is it about? Take notes.
Then choose **T** for **True** or **F** for **False**. 🔊 184

Notes

_____

_____

_____

_____

1. Mr. Giles enjoys gardening.   **T   F**
2. The girl makes complaints to Mr. Giles about what he's doing in the garden.   **T   F**
3. Mr. Giles doesn't want to help the bugs and the birds.   **T   F**

B Think about **A Beautiful Garden**. What is the girl's main complaint?
Choose the correct answer.

☐ a. Mr. Giles is making life difficult for the wildlife.

☐ b. There isn't any food for the birds.

☐ c. There isn't a bird bath.

C Listen to **A Beautiful Garden** again. Choose the correct answer. 🔊 185

1. What does Mr. Giles do every morning?

☐ a. He drinks coffee and watches the sun come up.

☐ b. He cuts the grass.

☐ c. He builds a bug hotel.

2. Why did Mr. Giles cut all the flowers?

☐ a. to decorate his house

☐ b. to grow grass

☐ c. to stop insects from coming into his garden

3. How often does Mr. Giles cut the grass?

☐ a. every day

☐ b. every month

☐ c. every week

4. Where do bugs and butterflies like to live?

☐ a. in the long grass

☐ b. in the vegetable garden

☐ c. in the bird bath

D Think about **A Beautiful Garden**. Answer the questions. Use full sentences.

1. What is the girl's first complaint?

   _____

2. What is the girl's reason for making her first complaint?

   _____

3. What is the girl's second complaint?

   _____

4. Why does the girl make a complaint about the bird feeder?

   _____

5. What two things does the girl suggest that Mr. Giles build or make?

   _____

6. What does Mr. Giles say he will do about the girl's complaints?

   _____

E Listen. Choose the correct answer. 🔊 186

1. You can make energy from nature by using **electricity** / **solar panels**.
2. Osman wanted to learn more about **pollution** / **the environment**.
3. Our teacher suggested we **reduce** / **recycle** the plastic we use.
4. Let's **reuse** / **recycle** this jar.
5. My grandfather's small village had no **recycling bins** / **electricity**.
6. How much do you care about **pollution** / **the environment**?

F Listen and read. Complete the sentences. 🔊 187

Our family has decided that we have to make a lot of changes if we really want to help the environment. So, last month, we bought a (1) _____ and some (2) _____ for our house. My dad says we still need to do more to (3) _____ the (4) _____ and the water we use every day. So now we watch a lot less television and have shorter showers! It's fun thinking of new ideas to help the planet!

Listen

LISTENING GOAL:
Listen for Reasons

Remember!
A **reason** explains why someone thinks the way they do. Listen for the word *because* to know someone's reason for their thinking.

A Listen to the radio interview **The Problem with Plastic**. What is it about? Take notes. Then choose the correct answer. 🔊 188

Notes

_____

_____

_____

1. What is the radio interview *The Problem with Plastic* about?

   ☐ a. how to recycle plastic   ☐ b. why a family picks up trash at the beach

2. How many people is Billy interviewing?

   ☐ a. 3   ☐ b. 4

B Think about **The Problem with Plastic**. Why does the Garza family pick up trash? Choose the correct answer.

   ☐ a. They put the trash into bags.

   ☐ b. It's dangerous for the sea animals and birds.

   ☐ c. They can reuse the plastic items.

C Listen to **The Problem with Plastic** again. Choose the correct answer. 🔊 189

1. The Garza family lives in the United States.

   ☐ a. true   ☐ b. false   ☐ c. doesn't say

2. The son's name is Billy.

   ☐ a. true   ☐ b. false   ☐ c. doesn't say

3. Plastic in the oceans kills about a million birds.

   ☐ a. true   ☐ b. false   ☐ c. doesn't say

4. Sea birds and sea animals eat plastic because they think it is food.

   ☐ a. true   ☐ b. false   ☐ c. doesn't say

5. The Garza family doesn't have a car.

   ☐ a. true   ☐ b. false   ☐ c. doesn't say

D Think about **The Problem with Plastic**. Complete the sentences with one, two, or three words.

1. The Garza family goes to a beach near their _____

2. They go to the beach every _____

3. They _____ some of the trash they find.

4. Most of the trash is _____

5. Plastic kills sea birds and sea _____

6. Mrs. Garza suggests turning off the lights and using _____ in your house.

E Listen and read. Choose the correct answer. 🔊 190

Last Saturday our (1) _____ broke. We couldn't fix it so we had to buy a new one. Dad rented a van to get it home because we couldn't (2) _____. We used a lot of (3) _____. Then, when we got home, Mom said we didn't need one and that we could hang the clothes outside, instead. So Dad took it back to the store. Then our (4) _____ started making funny noises.

1. ☐ a. dishwasher   2. ☐ a. take public transportation
   ☐ b. dryer   ☐ b. fit it in the car

3. ☐ a. electricity   4. ☐ a. dishwasher
   ☐ b. fuel   ☐ b. dryer

F Listen and complete the sentences. 🔊 191

1. Please don't forget to _____ when you leave.

2. Lucia always _____ when she has finished watering the garden.

3. I'm going to _____ this year.

4. We need to buy some _____

Speak

Remember!
Use apology phrases such as *I'm sorry* or *I apologize for* when you make an apology.

Circle the apology phrases. Then think of three new sentences using apology phrases. Tell your partner.

"I'm sorry," said Jae. "I forgot to turn off the light."

"That's OK," said mom. "Did you remember to shut off the water?"

"Oops!" said Jae. "I apologize for forgetting! I will remember next time."

UNIT 11

Listen

LISTENING GOAL:
Listen for Offers and Invitations

Remember!
An **offer** is when someone says they will help, give something, or do something. An **invitation** is a request to go somewhere. Listen for phrases like *Would you like* to identify offers and invitations.

A Listen to the announcement **A School Trip**. What is it about? Take notes. Then choose **T** for **True** or **F** for **False**. 🔊 192

Notes

_____

_____

_____

_____

1. The class is going on a school trip to San Francisco.   **T   F**
2. The students love the countryside.   **T   F**
3. The students will do activities in the countryside.   **T   F**

B Think about **A School Trip**. Which offers or invitations are made? Choose the correct answers.

☐ a. The teacher invites the class on a school trip.
☐ b. The teacher invites the students to climb a mountain.
☐ c. The teacher offers to show them a map.

C Listen to **A School Trip** again. Choose the correct answer. 🔊 193

1. Where is the school?
   ☐ a. downtown New York
   ☐ b. downtown San Francisco
   ☐ c. in the countryside

2. When is the school trip?
   ☐ a. tomorrow
   ☐ b. next week
   ☐ c. next month

3. What can the students do at the farm?
   ☐ a. learn about bats
   ☐ b. climb a mountain
   ☐ c. learn about chickens

4. Where can they learn about bats?
   ☐ a. at an exhibition
   ☐ b. at the lake
   ☐ c. at the workshop

D Think about **A School Trip** again. Answer the questions. Use full sentences.

1. What grade are the students in?

   _____

2. Where do the students think they might be going?

   _____

3. Where are they going first?

   _____

4. What can they do there?

   _____

5. How many students would like to climb the mountain?

   _____

6. What can the students do at the caves?

   _____

E Listen. Choose the correct answer. 🔊 194

1. Memet was really excited about visiting a **science museum** / **film studio**.
2. Last week Jia went to **a lecture** / **an exhibition** about Korean artists.
3. Would you like to go to a **food festival** / **concert** tomorrow?
4. Jason and his brother went **on a bus tour** / **to a lecture** yesterday.
5. Shireen went to **a lecture** / **an exhibition** to learn all about the ocean.
6. Toshi took a few photos when he went **on a bus tour** / **to a concert**.

F Listen and read. Complete the sentences. 🔊 195

Last week, on Aunt Shelley's birthday, we went to
(1) _____ about the International Space
Station. We both loved it so much that now we have tickets
to (2) _____ by an astronaut next weekend.
He's going to talk about the past, present, and future of
the space station. And on the way home from the lecture,
Aunt Shelley and I are going to (3) _____
because we can (4) _____ about life on the
moon. That sounds like the most fun of all!

Listen

LISTEN GOAL:
Listen for Refusals

Remember!
A **refusal** is saying *no* to an offer or an invitation. Listen for words and phrases like *Thank you, but* and *I'm sorry, but* to identify refusals.

A Listen to the story **A Competition**. What is it about? Take notes. Then choose the correct answer. 🔊 196

Notes

_____

_____

_____

1. What did Jamie really enjoy before he loved computers?
   ☐ a. science   ☐ b. sports

2. What does the girl think of her brother's love of computers?
   ☐ a. It's great.   ☐ b. It's boring.

B Think about **A Competition**. Which offers or invitations does Jamie refuse? Choose the correct answers.

☐ a. His friends invite him to play soccer.

☐ b. His teachers offer to help him with the competition.

☐ c. His uncle and aunt invite him on vacation.

C Listen to **A Competition** again. Choose the correct answer. 🔊 197

1. Jamie played soccer three times a week.
   ☐ a. true   ☐ b. false   ☐ c. doesn't say

2. Jamie is 17 years old.
   ☐ a. true   ☐ b. false   ☐ c. doesn't say

3. Jamie entered the video game competition.
   ☐ a. true   ☐ b. false   ☐ c. doesn't say

4. Jamie's computer game is about space travel.
   ☐ a. true   ☐ b. false   ☐ c. doesn't say

5. Jamie gave his prize to his sister.
   ☐ a. true   ☐ b. false   ☐ c. doesn't say

D Think about **A Competition**. Complete the sentences with one, two, or three words.

1. Jamie played basketball for the _____

2. Their uncle and aunt invited Jamie and his sister on _____

3. Jamie worked for _____ weeks on his idea.

4. The girl saw the competition poster in the _____

5. The second prize was a _____

6. The girl is thinking about entering the competition next _____

E Listen and read. Choose the correct answer. 🔊 198

I've never used a (1) _____ before, but I've read all about them online. They sound fun! My brother has a (2) _____ that he plays with all the time. And my mom has a (3) _____. But our favorite family activity is to (4) _____ and go hiking together.

1. ☐ a. virtual reality headset
   ☐ b. 3D printer

2. ☐ a. drone
   ☐ b. laptop

3. ☐ a. tablet
   ☐ b. smartwatch

4. ☐ a. write code
   ☐ b. be offline

F Listen and complete the sentences. 🔊 199

1. I use a _____ if I need help with my homework.

2. Anthony is always _____ in the evenings.

3. Frankie got a _____ for his birthday.

4. I'm learning how to _____ in my computer classes.

5. This _____ is really difficult to use.

6. My new _____ was very expensive.

Speak

Underline an offer. Circle an invitation. Then think of three new sentences using offers or invitations. Tell your partner.

Would you like a piece of cake?

Would you like to come to my house?

Would you like me to walk to school with you?

Dictionary

Definitions based on the *Oxford Basic American Dictionary for Learners of English.*

A

app *noun* a program that is designed to do a particular job: *a dictionary app*

B

beyond *preposition/adverb* on the other side of something; farther than something

boarding pass *noun* a card that you must show when you get on an airplane or a ship

bungee jump *verb* to jump from a high place, such as a bridge, with a thick elastic rope tied around your feet: *go bungee jumping*

bus tour *noun* a short visit by bus around a city, park, etc., usually in a group with someone who explains the things you see: *go on a bus tour*

C

candy store *noun* a store where candy is sold

carry-on luggage *noun* a small bag or case that you carry onto a plane with you

cave *verb* to go into caves under the ground as a sport: *go caving*

check-in *noun* the place where you go first when you arrive at an airport, to show your ticket, etc.

cheerful *adjective* happy

code *noun* a system of instructions for programming a computer: *write code*

concert *noun* a public performance of music: *go to a concert*

corner *noun* a place where two lines, walls, or roads meet: *around the corner/go to the corner*

courageous *adjective* brave

curious *adjective* having a strong desire to know about something

D

dangerous *adjective* likely to hurt someone

dead end *noun* a street that is only open at one end

delay *verb* to make someone or something late: *delayed*

dishwasher *noun* a machine that washes things like plates, glasses, knives, and forks

downtown *adverb* in or toward the center of a city, especially its main business area

drone *noun* a small aircraft without a pilot, controlled from the ground

dryer *noun* a machine for drying something

E

electricity *noun* power that comes through wires. Electricity can make heat and light, and makes machines work.

energy-saving light bulb *noun* a special light bulb that uses less electricity than a standard light bulb: *energy-saving light bulbs*

environment *noun* the air, water, land, animals, and plants around us

Europe *noun* the continent that is west of Asia and east of the Atlantic Ocean

exchange *verb* to give one thing and get another thing for it

exhibition *noun* a group of objects that are arranged in a museum, etc. so that people can look at them: *going to an exhibition*

F

fascinate *verb* to attract or interest someone very much: *fascinated*

festival *noun* a public event connected with a particular activity or idea, usually organized in the same place once a year: *went to a food festival*

film studio *noun* a place where movies are made: *visit a film studio*

first *adjective* before all others

fluent *adjective* able to speak easily and correctly

foolish *adjective* stupid or silly

fuel *noun* anything that you burn to make heat or power. Wood, gas, and oil are kinds of fuel.

Dictionary

G

German *adjective* from or connected with the country Germany

Germany *noun* a country in central Europe

gesture *noun* a movement of your head or hand to show how you feel or what you want

Greece *noun* a country in southeastern Europe

Greek *adjective* from or connected with the country Greece

grocery store *noun* a store where food and other small things for the home are sold

grow *verb* to plant something in the ground and take care of it: *grow your own vegetables*

H

hardware store *noun* a store where tools and equipment that are used to build or repair things in the house are sold

harness *noun* a set of bands that fasten something to a person's body

hilarious *adjective* very funny

hurry *verb* to move or do something quickly

I

immature *adjective* behaving in a way that is not sensible and is typical of younger people

impolite *adjective* not polite

intersection *noun* the place where two or more roads, lines, etc. meet and cross each other

L

lecture *noun* a talk to a group of people to teach them about something: *go to a lecture*

M

mother tongue *noun* the first language you learn to speak as a child

multilingual *adjective* able to speak more than one language

museum *noun* a building where people can look at old or interesting things: *visited a science museum*

O

offline *adverb* not using or connected to a computer or the Internet

on *preposition, adverb* used for showing where something is: *on the right*

on time *noun* not late or early

one-way *adjective* allowing travel in one direction only: *one-way street*

P

passport *noun* a small book with your name and photograph in it. You must take it with you when you travel to other countries

past *preposition, adverb* from one side to the other of someone or something; on the other side of someone or something: *go past*

polite *adjective* speaking or behaving in a way that shows respect

pollution *noun* dirty and dangerous chemicals, gases, etc. that harm the environment

popular *adjective* liked by a lot of people

public transportation *noun* buses and trains that everyone can use: *take public transportation*

R

raft *verb* to travel down a river on a raft: *go rafting*

recycle *verb* to do something to materials like paper and glass so that they can be used again

recycling bin *noun* a container for things that can be recycled

reduce *verb* to make something less

reuse *verb* to use something again or more than once

roller coaster *noun* a small train on a metal track that goes up and down and around bends, which people ride on for fun: *ride a roller coaster*

rope *noun* very thick, strong string

S

scuba dive *verb* to swim underwater using special equipment for breathing: *go scuba diving*

security *noun* the department of a company, a college, etc. that is responsible for protecting its buildings and people

shut off *phrasal verb* to stop a supply of electricity, water, or gas: *shuts off the water*

skydive *verb* to jump from a plane and fall through the air before opening your parachute: *go skydiving*

sleepy *adjective* tired and ready to sleep

smartwatch *noun* a watch that also has some of the functions of a computer

software *noun* programs for a computer

solar panel *noun* a piece of equipment on a roof that receives light and heat energy from the sun in order to make electricity or heat: *solar panels*

Southeast Asia *noun* an area of Asia that includes the countries Thailand, Vietnam, and Singapore

strange *adjective* unusual or surprising

 T

Thai *adjective* from or connected with the country Thailand

Thailand *noun* a country in southeastern Asia

3D printer *noun* a machine that uses information from a computer to make solid objects

toward *preposition* in the direction of someone or something

translate *verb* to change what someone has said or written in one language to another language

turn off *phrasal verb* to move the handle or switch that controls something, so that it stops: *turn off the light*

 U

unhappy *adjective* not happy

unkind *adjective* unpleasant and not friendly

up *preposition, adverb* in a certain direction: *up the street*

uptown *adjective* in or to the parts of a city or town that are away from the center, where people live

V

Vietnam *noun* a country in southeastern Asia

Vietnamese *adjective* from or connected with the country Vietnam

virtual reality headset *noun* a piece of equipment that you wear on your head in order to see pictures and sounds that are produced by a computer, and that are intended to seem almost like a real place or situation

 W

website *noun* a place on the Internet that you can look at to find out information about something: *go to a website*

workshop *noun* a time when people meet and work together to learn about something: *do a workshop*

worried *adjective* unhappy because you think that something bad will happen or has happened

Syllabus

Topic	Unit	Listening Goal	Key Words	Speaking Goal
TOPIC 1 **Where Am I?**	Unit 1	Listen for key information	*around the corner, dead end, downtown, go past, hurry, intersection, one-way street, uptown*	Give a speech
	Unit 2	Listen and take notes—Cornell Method	*beyond, candy store, first store on the right, go to the corner, grocery store, hardware store, toward, up the street*	Focus: Introduction sentences
TOPIC 2 **What Are They Like?**	Unit 3	Listen and analyze characters	*cheerful, curious, fascinated, foolish, impolite, polite, sleepy, unhappy*	Tell a fictional story
	Unit 4	Listen and make value judgments	*courageous, dangerous, hilarious, immature, popular, strange, unkind, worried*	Focus: Similes and metaphors
TOPIC 3 **Let's Talk!**	Unit 5	Listen and make inferences	*fluent, mother tongue, multilingual, Southeast Asia, Thai, Thailand, Vietnam, Vietnamese*	Summarize
	Unit 6	Listen and paraphrase	*dictionary app, Europe, German, Germany, gesture, Greece, Greek, translate*	Focus: Main ideas vs. details
TOPIC 4 **Fun in the Sun**	Unit 7	Listen for the speaker's purpose	*go bungee jumping, go caving, go rafting, go scuba diving, go skydiving, harness, ride a roller coaster, rope*	Give advice
	Unit 8	Listen for advice	*boarding pass, carry-on luggage, check-in, delayed, exchange, on time, passport, security*	Focus: Using *should*
TOPIC 5 **Our Beautiful Planet**	Unit 9	Listen for complaints	*electricity, environment, pollution, recycle, recycling bin, reduce, reuse, solar panels*	Make an apology
	Unit 10	Listen for reasons	*dishwasher, dryer, energy-saving light bulb, fuel, grow your own vegetables, shut off the water, take public transportation, turn off the light*	Focus: Using *I'm sorry* and *I apologize for*
TOPIC 6 **Let's Learn New Things!**	Unit 11	Listen for offers and invitations	*do a workshop, go on a bus tour, go to a concert, go to a food festival, go to a lecture, go to an exhibition, visit a film studio, visit a science museum*	Make offers and invitations
	Unit 12	Listen for refusals	*3D printer, drone, go to a website, offline, smartwatch, software, virtual reality headset, write code*	Focus: Using *Would you like*